Boss Up!

10 Traits One Must Have to Reach Self Actualization

BH

To: Shelli

Bryan Humphrey, MSW

Self Publish -n- 30 Days

This Is The Year For Your New Book

www.selfpublishn30days.com

Published by Self Publish –N– 30 Days

Copyright © 2018 Bryan Humphrey Speaks

Printed in the United States of America
ISBN: 978-1986486286

1. Motivation 2. Success – Psychological Aspects

Bryan Humphrey Speaks: BOSS UP!

Disclaimer/Warning:

TABLE OF
CONTENTS

ACKNOWLEDGMENT

I wish to express my sincere gratitude to my four wonderful parents; Vanessa Wesson, Claude Humphrey, Donald Wesson, and Yolanda Humphrey for providing me the foundation that I needed to enable my self-belief. I would like to thank the rest of my family members for always supporting me throughout my life journey.

I sincerely thank Dr. Alex Mwakikoti for convincing me to attain my Master's Degree at a young age. I also wish to express my gratitude to my fraternity brothers of Kappa Alpha Psi and other friends/consultants that have supported me along this journey to greatness, you know who you are.

I would like to thank my spiritual Father, God, for absolutely everything. He has me covered through the rain, sleet, and snow.

FOREWORD

Andrew Robinzine

Transforming the mind in a manner that is fit for your individual success is one of the hardest things that a person may encounter in the span of a lifetime. How can a person do that if they do not know that there is greatness within them that needs to be exposed? Mr. Bryan Humphrey is the bridge between that exterior doubt and that internal BEAST that's inside of you.

I've witnessed the man I first knew as "B-Hump" transform into the Mr. Bryan Humphrey that we see today. As a college student, B-Hump was submerged in the life instead of being submerged in himself. He indulged in alcoholism and immoral behaviors so much that it almost ruined his graduate school career setting him back a year and placing him on academic probation.

It was at this low moment that I first witnessed the switch in focus, but this focus was still not on "himself," it was a new focus on succeeding in school. He channeled this focus, and by the next graduating term his name was surely on that list. Being on that list though was not enough, he finished his last two semesters with a GPA of 4.0 and commendations from professors who thought he would not make it, as well as the dean of the college.

At this point, Bryan had achieved a milestone, graduating with his masters, but the next period of his life was sure to challenge his spiritual self. After graduating and moving back home, Bryan swiftly made the transition into corporate America after a brief three-month job search. Again, he fully invested himself in success at his workplace and not investing in "himself." He was very diligent in his profession and received compliments and commendations from his colleagues.

One day, arbitrarily, Bryan told me personally, "I don't love what I am doing, I will be quitting soon to focus more on my true dreams and goals." This came as a complete surprise to me, I had many questions, "To do what…. How are you…. What if…?" He responded that he knew what he was doing and that God had his back. This was one of the first times I've seen Bryan's full focus on, "himself." He said that he was going to inspire others the way that God has inspired him.

Since then, Bryan has been blessed to speak at women empowerment events, Churches, public schools, conferences, lounges, and other events.

Readers, get ready, you're about to be challenged beyond belief, your character will be in question, and you will begin to reevaluate your dreams. Are you truly ready for this challenge? Do you know what it means to, "BOSS UP," and if not are you ready to be receptive to direct criticism of what is holding you back? I challenge every reader to write down your setbacks before reading, "BOSS UP," and as you navigate from chapter to chapter, write down ways to fix those hindrances. Are you willing to do what it takes to reach your own self-actualization?

Mr. Bryan Humphrey is a perfect example of transformation, the man that will inspire men and women of all ages and backgrounds. Whether it is the struggling child or the prospering corporate executive, Mr. Humphrey has a message that is sure to reach all.

"You are chosen, you are special, , you are beautiful, you are cherished you are amazing people! ACT LIKE IT!"
—Bryan Humphrey

Enjoy, and BOSS UP!

PREFACE

Mr. Bryan Humphrey

Every person has the ability to reach their true greatness. Why? Because everybody was fearfully and wonderfully made in their own uniqueness. How? By having these 10 certain traits that I'm going to discuss in my book. However, what if grade school math was all wrong? What if a positive times a negative is really a positive? Positivity should be implemented in everything that you do.

As a social worker and a motivational speaker, it is my duty to change as many lives as I can for the better. This may sound cliché, but I remember while being in my first ever graduate school class at Stephen F. Austin State University, my professor, Dr. Freddie Avant, asked everyone in the class, "What do you plan to do with your Master's degree when you get it?" I answered, "I want to change the world," everybody looked at me awkwardly, I was only 22 years of age.

However, as I have gotten older, I have realized that pretty much everything starts with self-image. How you perceive yourself will always be more powerful than anybody else's opinion of you.

But on a deeper note, people always ask me why I have chosen this route of life. What have you been through? Why do you even care so much? When people ask me these questions, I smile real big and say, "If you only knew." Having the ability to sacrifice and adjust has transformed my life into such a peaceful, beautiful process. Once you understand how life really works, it gets pretty simple, yet still challenging, but simple.

So, what is self-actualization? Self-actualization is a term that is derived from the great Abraham Maslow. Abraham Maslow created the Maslow Hierarchy of Needs which explains the needs of life.

So let me break it down to you: basic needs must come first, things like food, water, rest, and warmth. Secondly, safety needs things like shelter and security. Thirdly, social; having friends and intimate relationships. Fourth, self-esteem, the status and feeling of achievement. Lastly, at the top, like the very top is self-actualization. Self-actualization is becoming who and what you truly want to become. According to numerous studies, they say only one percent of individuals on this earth reach self-actualization.

So, what is the problem? Why do most of the people on this earth don't want to be what they truly desire to be? To sum it all up, they really don't know how. And that's ok, that's why I have written this book to get you back into the groove of things; the groove to go after your wildest and scariest dreams. What are you waiting for? There will never be a perfect time, so you might as well start now!

I'm going to let you guys know now that I am not perfect at all, and nobody is. However, I am a person who is very aware of himself, which allows me to understand life in it's simplistic of forms. Just from observation, most individuals have one or two unhealthy habits that are holding them back from reaching their full potential. I will admit I have gotten over mine; it was extremely challenging, but worth it. I really enjoyed drinking alcohol and being a player for a good portion of my life. I utilized those things as ways to cope with my life. I'm not going to lie, it had gotten really bad. I was more than just a "social drinker." I was drinking every single day and at the most randomness of times.

I couldn't slow down with the women! Some were dating other men, but at that time, it didn't matter to me. The lifestyle continued even after I got my master's degree and had a good paying job working for the state. However, I just knew that something didn't feel right. For instance, why didn't my professional achievements align with my lifestyle? Something felt really backward to me.

I felt lost, even while having a lovely apartment, decent credit score, two cars in my name and a clean criminal background. I still felt lost. Was it my job? Was it my environment? Was it my group of friends? Was it my family? Nope, it was me! I was lost.

I have never seen my father even drink a lick of alcohol in my life, so where did I learn this behavior from? Both of my parents are remarried and in faithful and committed relationships.

So, why did I choose to be a player? I was raised in the church house, so why was I becoming so judgmental about other people? Did I really think success was about everything on the outside? Well, to let you guys know, true growth and development start on the inside. You can only fake and pretend so long.

I no longer drink alcohol, I'm not a player anymore, and I welcome all types of individuals with open arms. So when I tell you to "Boss Up," I just don't mean getting degrees, good paying jobs, getting married, or starting your own successful business. It's deeper than that. Don't get me wrong, all of those things are great and will increase your self-esteem.

However, when I say "Boss Up," I also mean to overcome your deepest fears, break those unhealthy habits, go after what you truly want, and develop a strong sense of self-love and appreciation for yourself that not one single soul can break.

It's time to get real about "your" life and become the person that you truly want to become. You are already the person you want to become, you just have to bring it out of you. Boss Up!

FAITH

Hebrews 11:1- Now faith is the substance of things hoped for and the evidence of things not seen. It feels that the best things worth having are the things we had no earthly idea of how to get it once we started going after it. We are humans, so of course, we want to be sure of everything. However, the beauty of life comes from the unknown. It comes from the setbacks, challenges, downfalls, bad decisions, and crazy sacrifices.

I remember when I left my job working for the state in May of 2017, my coworkers at the time was like, "Bryan you're actually leaving?" Like why? One of my coworkers at the time asked me, "So how are you going to do it? Like, find a job before you run out your savings. I remember when I left a job it took me five months to find another one." I looked him dead in his face and said, "I know my value, and I'll be just fine."

I know individuals that will go to church Sunday, but when something happens in their life where they don't seem to be in control of it, they go ballistic. They start questioning God like, why? Why me? Having real faith begins with trust. So why did I leave a job making right under 60k with 401k, retirement, and health insurance with nothing lined up?

It was nothing but faith. Faith is having the confidence that you are going to get through the situation that you're in without knowing when your blessing is coming. The funny thing was that one day, I had a job interview and the lady interviewing me stated, "You left your job without no job security? Why would you do something like that?" I looked at her dead in her face and said, "I know my value, and I know my worth." Pretty much the same thing I said to my former coworker.

The reason why I left working for the state was because I wanted to start working on my dreams and personal goals more intensely. The job I had working for the state was emotionally draining me, and it had almost changed my beliefs about life.

So, what actually happened? Did I prevail overall, or did I fail like most people expected me to do? In short, I ended up starting a job exactly one month after I left working for the state that matched my resume completely. The flexibility of the job and the organization's purpose was another reason why I took it.

Of course, sacrifices had to be made, like extra paperwork, working on weekends, clients canceling/rescheduling visits, but by the grace of God, I was put in a position to go after what I truly wanted in life. Even though it paid less than the state, I was now given the opportunity to start investing in myself and living out my true purpose on a serious basis. It was now time to BOSS UP!

Faith is such a beautiful concept of life. Faith is not just a noun. I believe faith is a verb. When you act on your faith consistently, it literally changes the whole ballgame. When faith is talked about, it isn't a subject just for churchgoing individuals. This is a subject that every single person on this earth can learn from. Faith allows you to attack challenging situations without breaking down mentally.

Have you ever heard someone say, "This isn't going to work out" or, "We are not going to get anywhere with this?" If you have, you know how ugly it sounds when people say it. As soon as you hear someone saying something like this, just remove yourself from the situation because negativity will be transcended to you subconsciously. Some individuals do not have much faith; like at all, it's ridiculous.

Then they have the nerve to call people that are living well lucky, arrogant, selfish, and all types of crazy stuff. However, the weird thing is, you do have to be a little crazy to remain faithful.

Faithful over few, ruler over all. But what does this really mean? I was in school from age four to age 25 and ended up being the first person in my family to achieve a master's degree. However, you really think I was just doing this for myself? You think I went through seven years of college non-stop just for my own personal growth? You're sadly mistaken. When it comes to reaching self-actualization, the purpose of what you do must always be more important than what you do.

My goal was to break a cycle in my family and to show my loved ones that it's possible to achieve anything you set your mind to when you express true faith. I have never seen any individual in my family ever do it, so how did I do it? I didn't know anyone in my personal life that I hung out with that had a master's degree, so how did I do it? It was faith - the evidence of things hoped for and the evidence of things "not" seen.

I'm a very observant individual, and over time, I've learned that the strongest people that I've ever come in contact with have made some crazy sacrifices. For instance, I invested nearly my entire overtime check from my state job into a new laptop, new camera, marketing tools, and other things for my speaking brand.

Did it hurt? Heck yes! I could have gone on a vacation with that money, a lovely vacation. However, having faith allowed me to go forth with something I knew would fall into place over time. Faith is never about being perfect. Faith is about knowing that the pieces of the puzzle will match perfectly in due time. Bill Gates once stated, "You can't connect the dots looking forward, you can only connect them looking backward. So you have to trust that the dots will somehow connect in your future. You have to trust in something – your gut, destiny, life, karma, whatever."

You want to reach self-actualization, but you don't trust yourself. The first mistake some individuals make is, they pursue something without trusting themselves. Trusting yourself takes time, but you must trust before true faith is manifested. I remember a speech I did at my mother's church one time; I stated to the crowd, "Some of y'all come to church every Sunday, Bible study, scream and shout, but your faith is wack." Kind of harsh, right? However, it's sad, but true.

Some individual's faith are wack. If you're reading this book and your faith isn't where it needs to be, I don't mean to hurt your feelings, but I want you to be aware of how you are really living. One of the first rules to reaching self-actualization is to never lie to self. You won't be able to trust yourself along your process if you are lying to yourself. Great things are rewarded to individuals that stay true.

Having faith brings peace. When you are sure that the result will be good, and things will fall in place, you don't rush the process. It allows you to embrace all the nonsense that life brings you along your way. Always remember, if it doesn't kill you, it only makes you stronger.

Practicing a faithful lifestyle brings you strength and understanding. It allows you to see life from such a beautiful and grateful perspective. It allows you to laugh at yourself when you make a silly mistake. It allows you to stand still sometimes. It allows you to take a little break and spend time with your family and friends. Having faith will enable you to pursue your goals in a relaxed manner. The more you practice true faith, the more you will be able to handle the reward once obtained. Whatever that reward maybe.

We wonder what really makes individuals faithful to something, especially when they are unsure of the result. Has anyone ever called you crazy or weird? If they have, then look at it as a good thing. How can you achieve crazy things without being crazy?

Having true faith can allow you to miss out on a lot of fun or instant gratification. Think about the guy that always blows money on drinks and going out. He is probably having a bunch of fun at the certain moment. However, what happens later down the line when this person loses his car, job, or doesn't have a good enough credit score to own not a darn thing?

When you remain faithful to something, it enables you to look at life from a longitudinal perspective. You will know that the sacrifices you make today will allow you to grow tomorrow.

Reaching self-actualization can be tricky because it's easy to get confused about the people that have really reached it. You cannot reach self-actualization without staying faithful to your process. Why do you think there are high school football stars that go off to big Division 1 universities to play ball on a full scholarship and they are right back home after their first year of college because of their choices? They didn't stay faithful to the sport.

It could have been a possibility that they got caught up with the parties, women, drugs, and so on. And their chances of playing professionally one day had started to dwindle down.

Staying faithful is simple but difficult. In fact, sometimes it can be very difficult, but it doesn't have to be. Think about one of the greatest athletes of all time, Michael Jordan; he didn't make the varsity basketball team until his senior year of high school. Even though he didn't make the cut the previous year, he remained faithful and became an absolute monster at North Carolina and then in the NBA. Just by him staying faithful, they have created a clothing and shoe brand under his name, Jordan.

While I was in graduate school at Stephen F. Austin State University, I used to look on social media and see my high school buddies living life man; going to crazy vacations, buying their first home, having their first child, and getting engaged. And I'm in grad school busting my butt to get it. However, I didn't allow other people's lives to steer me off my path. I surely could have, but didn't.

Did getting a master's degree help me reach self-actualization? No, it didn't. But the professional skills I learned while in grad school has enabled me to be so smooth and productive in the real world. I don't care how hard something may be in my professional life, I believe that I have the skills to make it look easy. Now that's how you Boss Up!

Remaining faithful allows you to get to the destination quicker. Being zoned in on what you truly desire to be and valuing delayed gratification will separate you from others. While in my early 20s, I learned that the more I think long term about the decisions I make, the faster I will become the person that I truly desire to be.

Average people will make decisions based on how they feel not what's best.

Average people say things like this, "We got all the time in the world to grow up," "Who cares bro just have fun," and "Tomorrow isn't promised." And they actually get to tomorrow and realize they are late on their dreams and their bills. Average people are not faithful, with average people it's always something. Either they are lying about something, they are lazy, they are inconsistent, they are tardy, they are making excuses, and all the other disarray of things. You cannot reach self-actualization with an average mindset. If you think you still can, please go sit down somewhere.

Is faith measured? Why does it seem easy for some people to be faithful to a cause, a dream, in a relationship, improving their business, and for others, it appears extremely difficult? Having the characteristic of being faithful is something we must learn to do. For some children, it becomes more natural to do because they see their parents sticking to the process regardless of what happens along the way. And for other children, they are raised in complete dysfunction and by inconsistent individuals. So when these children meet someone who is absolutely faithful to the process of anything, it appears weird and crazy to them. People learn to be faithful in different forms and fashions. However, it is easier to learn unfaithful habits than faithful habits.

People call me crazy all the time, like literally. Why do they? Because I am. People who are bossing up and headed towards self-actualization will seem crazy to most. Then people will question you saying, "Are you really going to do that?" "Do you even know the right people?" "Do you have enough money for those big dreams?" and so on and so forth.

Developing faithful habits towards your wildest dreams starts in the mind. Your mind literally controls your process. When you are faithful in a couple of areas in your life, it makes it much easier to become faithful in other areas of your life. Don't believe me... try it. By me being faithful to my family, working out 5-6 days a week for the past decade, faithful to self-educating myself, and faithful to praying every day has enabled me to be faithful to my dream on such a strong degree.

When chasing success, life itself gets challenging. Being faithful isn't always being faithful to a person (spouse) or the process (dream), but it also means being faithful to you, yes I said you. Being faithful to yourself allows you to put your needs first. It allows you to take care of yourself. When you are faithful to yourself, you feel good about yourself. When you feel good, you do good. When you feel good, you can project that beautiful things are going to happen in your life longer down the road. Once self-actualization is reached, you will feel darn good.

Being faithful enables you to be in control of your life. You won't be able to control every situation that arises in your life. If you think you can, then you got some soul searching to do. Yes, you can be in control of yourself when you're not in control of the situation. Life is ten percent of what happens to you and ninety percent of how you respond to it. Once you recognize that you can't control everything, you begin to react differently. You react in such a secure manner that you know everything will be fine.

Even if the situation didn't conclude in the fashion that you wanted it to, you still were fine because you're at peace. You must believe that everything happens for a reason to be at peace. There is a positive concept that can be learned out of every single situation that happens in your life. Yes, even those situations that provoked you to have harsh and negative thoughts. My stepdad, Donald Wesson, actually told me this while we were sitting down on the couch one day, "Deep down inside, everybody wants peace, don't get fooled."

Being faithful to the process makes you a stronger person. It makes you more self-discipline, more trustworthy, and a more reliable person. Having faith allows you to keep your cool when nothing is going your way. To stay on track on your journey to self-actualization, your lifestyle must mirror faithfulness. You don't have to be perfect, just stay true. Boss Up!

LOVE

What's love got to do with it? Love is the strongest wave anybody can surf on. Where do love and self-actualization connect? Well, let's be clear, how can anything be prosperously done without love? Love allows one to look over the negative, ugly, bad, and harshness of a situation or person and see the good in it. Working directly with at-risk children and families has taught me a lot about life. It has forced me to love stronger. The reason I say this is because "Love is unconditional."

Love is never conditional. Like is conditional, lust is conditional, trust is conditional, and hate is conditional. There are other things that are conditional as well. But love, genuine love is the only thing that will allow an individual to stick it through the worst of times along their journey to greatness.

Love is already strong. Love isn't weak; it's not off and on. Love allows you to push through the most negative situations just because the purpose of what you do outweighs the product that comes out from what you do. I know we often hear people say, "Do what you love." But what if what you love doesn't pay you much, what if it doesn't take you on the vacations you want to go on, what if it doesn't allow you to buy the kind of car you want, what if love, yes love, doesn't even allow you to love yourself.

Then, is it really worth doing what you love? But remember, "Love is unconditional." I have heard numerous individuals quit doing what they loved to do because it didn't bring immediate gratification. However, here is the reason why most individuals quit chasing their dreams. They are not chasing it the right way. Yep. That's got to be it.

For example, just because you love helping people doesn't mean you have to go into the field of social work, just because you love teaching people doesn't mean you have to go into the field of public/private education, just because you love fixing things doesn't mean you have to be a mechanic, just because you love making other people look good doesn't mean you have to be a barber, and so on.

Sometimes as humans, we let labels, field of work, college majors, type of degrees define who we are. But that is so false; you define who you are!

Love overcomes any fear. What if your best friend was in a house that is on fire and you were scared as heck of fires? Would you go in and try to rescue them? If you loved them, you would. There is no probably or maybe to it. We must attack our life purpose in the same fashion.

If what we do is what we love, then it is inevitable to dig deep and boss up through the scariest of situations. I wish I could say it's going to be easy, but it won't be because "Love is unconditional."

Your purpose for what you do is more powerful than what you do. Real purpose comes from love. If you don't truly love what you do, your purpose will be lackadaisical. Purpose strengthens when you strengthen it. For example, have you ever met someone helping people on a daily basis and is making a bunch of money from it? If you have, take a good look at that person. I'm pretty sure they strengthen their purpose.

The harder it is to break you, the more valuable you will become. Love isn't fake. You cannot fake the process. You cannot fake life. The more you pretend, the more you push yourself away from becoming the person you truly want to become.

To love is to know. Know where you are exactly at along your process. Know how long you have gone and how long it will take to get to where you are going. When you are confused or misunderstood about your current state, it stretches the process.

The quickest way to get to where you are going is to understand why you are where you are. The more you know yourself, the more you will know your journey. And the more you know your journey, the more you will trust the process. The process is what it is my brothers and sisters. If you love it, you'll stick it through. If you don't, you will get exposed. I'm pretty sure you don't want to get exposed as a fake or fraud.

That's why I am here to encourage and empower you to be the real you. Love your current state because love braces appreciation. If you're not grateful for what you have now, then do you really deserve more? Love increase patience. Love allows you to feel good about where you are in the process, and the more you feel good about something, the more you will be willing to wait for it.

Keep your enemies closer. You cannot keep your enemies closer if you don't express love. Why is keeping your enemies close important to reaching self-actualization? It is important because your enemies will either break you or make you. If you don't express love to your enemies, then you will become just like them. Misery loves company. It makes them feel better when they can breach the deficiencies out of you. However, if you approach the situation with love, you will be fine. Love will always be stronger than hate. Being hateful of others, you have to deal with, and being hateful of situations you must go through; to reach greatness will suck all the life out of you. "Love is unconditional."

I gave up certain things when I started to love myself truly. The more you understand yourself the easier it will be to love yourself. I gave up alcohol because alcohol was my escape goat to life. Alcohol allowed me to cope with life. I wasn't just a social drinker, I was an everyday drinker. It didn't matter the occasion. Now some may read this and say, "I drink all the time and I am perfectly fine," but you have to remember I am different from you. What held me back may not hold you back. I am just speaking from my perspective. However, from the bottom of your heart, you know what's really slowing you down. I knew drinking was slowing me down intrinsically, so I stopped. Real change comes from the inside out.

Love leads to obsession, or is it the other way around? To reach self-actualization, one must be obsessed with what they do, but on a deeper note. One must be even more obsessed with the purpose of what they do. I'm obsessed with improving other people's lives that's why I literally don't get burnt out of serving others.

The more you fall in "love" with the service of what will help you reach self-actualization, the more straight your route to achieving it will be. This is what you called clarity. Being clear about what you want to become and why you want to become it gives you so much power. Once attained, this power will enable you to boss up and do whatever it takes to reach greatness. When you love something, you go crazy about it; it's even hard to stop thinking about it. You want to know why? It's because love is an emotion, it's a feeling. The subconscious part of your brain controls the paradigm which enforces the habits you have.

I have a habit and true obsession with bettering people's lives. It's not something that I even have to think about to do. I just do it, like Nike. Every person on this earth is obsessed with something, whether it's a sport, a tv show, working out, church, praying, shopping, making money, speaking, their spouse, their children, reading, and so on. I truly believe every single individual on this earth is crazy about something. They might not admit to it, but that's nothing but love.

"They hate to love me." Y'all remember Terrell Owen's famous line when he played in the NFL, it was a classic right. However, this is similar to the process that you're going through right now. Sometimes you will hate the process, not because you're not doing what you love, but because you sometimes hate things that come with it. We loved how T.O. played wide receiver in the pros, but sometimes his actions and comments off football field weren't as applauding. I have made so many sacrifices and adjustments in my life I have been accustom to. Do I honestly like changing up my patterns of how I do things here and there? Absolutely not, but I do it because I love what I am doing for others.

By just changing my lifestyle and breaking some of my unhealthy habits like drinking every day and messing around taken women allowed others to see the change in my life. This showed others that I wasn't playing any games and I was serious about my own personal growth. Sometimes you will have to give up something you love to become someone you love. And when I first started on the journey to breaking those two unhealthy habits,

I absolutely hated it, my body hated it, my mind hated it, but my spirit didn't.

My spirit didn't because I made a vow to do it, and there is nothing stronger than your spirit. Your soul is extremely powerful when utilized properly. So yes, even though we hated T.O. sometimes we loved his spirit.

Love is such a beautiful thing. And no, I don't mean an Instagram post of a couple driving off from their wedding in a car that isn't theirs. What I mean is the genuineness you have for what you do. You don't let anything get in your way of loving what you do. You protect your dreams and goals with all thine heart and soul. Love increases intensity. Love allows you to remain serious along your journey to greatness even when everybody around you is laughing at you for dreaming so big. But you know what? Let them haters hate and express love to them anyway. Once you are ok with showing love to your haters even when they laugh in your face, then they will know that they can't destroy your spirit. When you love yourself, you protect yourself. When you love what you do, you protect what you do.

You know when you don't love what you do. Don't play yourself; you know boo boo. Do you think it's possible to develop a love for something that you don't enjoy doing at first? Yes, you absolutely can. The love for something isn't built overnight. However, it shouldn't take you forever and a day to find out if you do. The more time you put into something, the more you will realize if it's for you or if it isn't. And yes, sometimes that timeframe is longer than expected, but still doesn't take forever. If you want to be the top 1-2% of individuals on this earth, then I highly suggest you start doing what you love.

If you don't know what you love just yet, then start doing things that you enjoy, but more intensely, then you will figure out eventually. You should love what you do so much that it's like a craving. A craving like my mother's shepherd's pie. When you crave to do something, it enhances the desire to do it. And desire leads to actions.

Action is crucial to your success and you reaching greatness. Love can make you nervous and even uncomfortable, but it won't stop you from doing what you set your mind to. To all reading this book, I know you may be scared as heck to make that next move along your journey to reaching self-actualization, but always remember: make your next move your best move.

I wouldn't say life is like a game of chess, but if you're going to play the game of becoming what you truly want to become, you better go for that kingpin! You got this, trust yourself, love yourself.

There is no such thing as over-love. If you have been given the blessed opportunity to do what you love on a consistent basis, then you should absolutely embrace that. Yes, I understand we all need breaks here and there, but if you are doing what you love, then naturally you shouldn't want to stay away from it too long. Some people say real love always finds its way back. Well, if we took this same approach to our dreams and goals, then why are most of us not achieving what we truly desire?

The answer to that is lack of focus. I mean, come on now, would you rather be laser-focused or off and on? Would you trust someone who is utterly zoned it with pursuing his passion or someone who goes on unnecessary vacations every two to three months? Trust builds love, and vice versa. The more others trust you with the position of greatness, the more you will continue to love it. Some people are not loving what they do anymore because they don't appear trustworthy to others. For example, when I go speak to a couple of hundred high school seniors who are graduating high school soon, that principal of the school is trusting me to deliver a message that is going to leave a profound impact on them. Would you continue to love what you do if nobody even trusted you doing it?

Being the first in the family to achieve something brings a lot of pressure. I am the first person in my family to achieve a master's degree first to become a public speaker, and the first person to become an author.

For most, this would be too much pressure, but I love pressure. Like, come one dude bring it! If you are going to love something, you better love everything that comes with it, and yes the most frightening stuff. You have to remember "love is unconditional." If love was supposed to feel good, then everybody would reach self-actualization. However, the truth is, loving what you do and everything that comes with it can suck at times.

You will question yourself, you will doubt yourself, you will feel nervous, you will not be as confident at times, and you will get angry. I'm telling you, it will most definitely happen. Pursuing anything great can make you feel like a total crap sometimes, but is it worth it that we do? I believe so.

Love has no end point, breaks, yes. Take your breaks, it's good to celebrate your accomplishments. However, have you ever wondered why people who are living out their purpose never stop doing what they are doing until they die?

Think about greats like Bob Proctor, Oprah Winfrey, Warren Buffett, and Dr. Eric Thomas, they are still bossing up and making a difference in this world and they all have been doing what they have been doing for plenty of years! Why don't individuals that have reached self-actualization just retire and be normal like everybody else. It's because they can't, they are absolutely obsessed with what they do.

I am obsessed with bettering your life, if I wasn't you think I would actually take the time out my busy day to write this book? Come on now, there's no way! Love brings obsession and in order to win at what you do on a consistent basis, you must be obsessed with it.

Lastly, love allows you to fight. It allows you to fight for what you feel is right. You must fight for what you truly desire. This world is not going to give it you by a long shot. I had to fight for my master's degree when I nearly got kicked out of grad school after my third semester.

I had to beg my professors to give me another shot. They did, and I won. I won the fight. You can't win the fights that you never choose to fight. If you don't love what you are pursuing, your fight won't be as strong and it'll be easy to give up. So, love what you do. Boss Up!

CONFIDENCE

Self-belief is the best belief. Don't let mediocre individuals make you feel bad for believing in yourself so much. I met with one of my undergraduate professors, Dr. Mwakikoti, about 6 months after I earned my master's degree from Stephen F. Austin State University. And while we were discussing our greatness he stated, "Bryan, you always believed yourself, and sometimes it was to a level that was over the roof. I was like this young man really believes in himself and that's good, but we have to remember to be realistic as well."

People who reach self-actualization don't live in a fantasy world and aren't magical creatures, they are individuals who saw through their vision and made it happen. If some people are not feeling slightly uncomfortable around you, then you probably don't believe in yourself enough.

Is confidence something that you are born with or is it something that you learn? It's something you learn. I remember in high school my friends and I went to the mall on weekends and tried to meet girls and hopefully get their number. My friend Jerome Roberts used to call me "ruthless" because I started to not care about if I would get rejected or not and I went for the win anyways. Well, of course I got rejected plenty of times, but I did win sometimes as well. By doing this over and over again, it gave me true confidence. Noticed, I said true, not some flaky confidence.

My friend Jerome told everybody at football practice the following Monday, "Yo Bryan don't care about getting rejected, he is about that life." You cannot tiptoe into your greatness. You are going to have to dig deep and come with it full force my brothers and sisters. Life is serious business and if you don't believe that you are a business, you won't win in business.

Consistency builds confidence. It definitely takes more time to build confidence in certain things than in others. I remember when I first became a part of the greatest fraternity in the world, Kappa Alpha Psi, I was so nervous shimmying! My heart was beating fast as heck, I was like oh no.

However, over time I began to get more comfortable with myself doing it, and it became a breeze. I have been working out consistently for the past 15 years of my life. So I developed a strong habit of going to the gym and it feels so good when I pump the iron. Once confidence is built in doing something, the next step is making that something a habit. Working out for me is a habit. I don't think twice about doing it, I just do it like Nike.

When you first start seriously pursuing your purpose in life, it can be scary and uncomfortable. However, I believe that in those scary and uncomfortable times, growth is made. Prosperity is developed to doing things in confidence. If you are going to do it, do it big then.

Confidence leads to creation. Being confident allows you to try new things along your journey to greatness. Everything isn't going to always work. Being confident enables the 60-year-old barbershop owner to make an Instagram and Facebook fan page to promote his business more effectively. Being confident enables you to do what "works" not just what you are used to. Confidence doesn't fear change, if change is necessary for growth.

Also, confidence allows you to admit that what you're trying to do isn't working, or isn't working anymore. Being confident in whatever you do allows you to bring the Boss out of you. Confidence enabled me to leave a 60k job working for the state to pursue my true purpose of life. The reason is because the purpose of what you do is more important than what you do. If you are doing something for the wrong reasons, it will flaw your confidence.

Real confidence is solid. Real confidence is genuine. Real confidence is relentless. Real confidence is you. My brothers and sisters, you know deep down inside you are Boss! So why you playing?

Being confident will make others who believe in you feel better about themselves. Have you noticed why certain individuals just attract so many people around them? When you truly believe in yourself, you will be a token unto others who don't really believe in themselves or that are trying to develop the characteristic of believing in themselves. Believe, believe, believe! You have to believe. Pursuing something consistently without believing in yourself is totally redundant. Don't deteriorate your own greatness because you don't believe that you are not good enough.

My brothers and sisters, you are good enough. You are worth it. You are chosen. You are valued. You are cherished. You are special. You are amazing people.

When everybody else said no, don't do it. Say to yourself, "I got this." Saying self-positive statements to reaffirm your confidence is totally a good thing. Talking to yourself can help you gain clarity of things which enhance your confidence. I learned the habit of talking to myself from my father.

Even though it appears weird to be in the grocery store talking out loud without any headphones in, it actually makes me feel more confident about whatever I am going through. We have to understand that there are processes in the process and everybody's process is going to be different in some fashion.

Feeling better about the small processes can help you stay focused to reach the big goals. I truly believe that one of the main reasons most individuals don't go after what they truly desire is because they believe that they don't have what it takes to achieve the goal at hand. But you do. I know you do.

Not having patience can really deteriorate your confidence. I used to struggle with being inpatient because I believe I'm great at everything I do. So I believed that I deserved the glory as soon as people found out how great I was. But here is the catch to success; it is not always all about performance, it's also about being mentally tough to deal with everything that comes with the glory.

Once I realized my lack of patience was depleting my confidence, I learned to be grateful where I was at and respected that things take time. Being patient shows that you are in control and being in control reaps confidence.

Staying confident onto your journey of reaching self-actualization will help you boss up through the nonsense, the rejections, and the no's. When you are truly confident, you embrace the no's. When someone tells me no, I'm like, "Ok cool everything happens for a reason." So now it's my time to find the reason why I got told no and go even harder to show the people who told me no that they made the wrong decision.

Confident individuals are problem solvers. The more problems you can solve, the more success you will have. While throwing events in grad school with my New Elite brothers Romeo Gabana and Ricquan Williams, we learned the problem of why nobody was cashing out anymore. So we utilized our confidence to make the sacrifice to fill in the gaps that others feared to do. We found the problem, found out why it was a problem, brainstormed over possible solutions, tried the top solutions, fixed the problem and boom! Greatness existed. Greatness comes from believing that you have what it takes to make a difference in whatever you do. I know you have what it takes. The question is, do you?

You know you're a boss! Just believe it. Know thyself, love thyself. When I was joining Kappa Alpha Psi, my Dean, David Malveaux, said to me very assertively, "Nobody cares how smart you are if you are not confident." That comment he made to me held so much power and anointing. So why do we meet smart people and they are not winning in life? Why do some seem to struggle just as much as people who struggled in school?

Well, I know for sure the lack of confidence is one of them. They say A and B students end up working for C and D students. Well, this could go both ways, but without expressing confidence along your journey to greatness, it will make it very difficult to accomplish pretty much anything in this day of age.

How can you sell yourself to a potential buyer, a CEO, a lady or man you're interested in, or even people around you without being confident? People who are starting new trends must be confident! They are bringing something new to the table! If you are creating your own personal brand like myself, you'll have to convince others why you are so special. Like, what makes you different from others?

If you are having an issue with developing confidence, you might need to get around more environments that will require you to be confident. Placing yourself in uncomfortable situations will enable you to be stretched. Being stretched is a good thing. When you are getting stretched, you are becoming better which will lead to you having more confidence.

You will lose some friends and gain more haters when your confidence is getting stronger. Average people don't like to feel uncomfortable. Be careful who you surround yourself with, there is a bunch of average people out there.

Me personally, I set strict boundaries when dealing with average people. It's nothing personal; it's just that I know where I am taking my life and I don't want to make you feel less than around me, so I will limit myself around you. Don't be afraid of being the best you or even being a better you. You deserve it!

Difficult experiences will build confidence or break it. Don't be broken. I remember when I got placed on academic probation while being in graduate school; that same semester, I quit my hotel job, got into a car wreck, and lost my good friend of mine, Qudus Jacobs passed away. Yes, all this happened in one semester. Rest in Peace King, 187.

However, I pressed on. I pressed on to my way to greatness. That semester, I finished up on the Dean's list, got off academic probation, and bought me a new car. I really felt good about myself entering my last year of grad school.

That spring 2015 semester made me. My last year of graduate school I made all A's, was awarded a scholarship from the T. L. L. Temple Foundation in Lufkin, Texas, my New Elite brothers and I threw three very financially successful college parties and became the first person in my family to achieve a master's degree ever. Thank you, Stephen F. Austin State University Masters of Social Work Program, for creating a monster!

Confidence brings freedom; spiritual freedom, personal freedom, and financial freedom. When you truly believe that you deserve more, that's when you will get more. You are not getting what you desire, or going after what you desire because deep down inside you don't believe you deserve it yet. But you do, you really do.

Rich people aren't happy, free people are. Having a sense self-control over your career, business, family, health, finances, and most importantly yourself is quite important to gaining freedom. Just know you are worth more. No, you are not being greedy, so stop, tell yourself that and live a life of self-fulfillment and merit. Having confidence will help you to tear those walls down blocking you from your greatness.

Confidence brings faith. Confidence will permit you to stop being a scary cat and take that jump onto the next platform of your life. Confidence will allow you to continuously go into environments where you are unwelcomed to prove your point. Confidence equals crazy. If you want to achieve your wildest dreams or just be secure enough to live a healthy life, then you best be crazy about something.

Some individuals are crazy about their spouse, their children, their business, their car, their home, their shoes, their church, their community, and so on. When you are crazy about something, you will do whatever it takes to develop the confidence to keep that something going.

Just keep pushing. I remember one of the first speeches I spoke at Fort Worth Western Hills high school, thanks to Mrs. Vanita

Bell. I told the graduating seniors, "When you wake up every morning, just look in the mirror and tell yourself 'I'm beautiful.'" You are beautiful beyond measure, beyond limits, yes you. Every day comes with its own trials and tribulations, but every time you look in the mirror, just tell yourself you're beautiful no matter how great or harsh your day has been. You know you rock the boat. You know you can't be stopped. You know you a King and Queen. You are God's highest form of creation. Please act like it.

Life is too beautiful itself for you not to be walking around feeling good about self. And if you are dealing with something tough that's delaying your process, don't worry, just keeping moving boldly and eventually that wall that was once in front of you will gladly break down for you.

Everybody doesn't act confidently, but everybody has the ability to be confident. You were born great! I truly believe that reaching self-actualization starts with knowing that you are capable of doing, not necessarily knowing how, but knowing along your journey that you have the strength to make whatever needs to happen to take your life to the next level. You are next level.

Sometimes when I don't feel my best, I tell myself, "Bryan you better Boss Up because you know you're next level, stop playing games." I get caught talking to myself in numerous places like the gym, grocery store, mall, gas station, and even while I'm hanging out with some of my friends.

Self-talk may not be for everyone, but it has increased my confidence tremendously. When the world is trying to knock you down, its good to tell yourself positive things like "I got this," "I can do this," "Man, this is going to be a breeze," "Trust yourself king," "Just keep on pushing," and "You are worth it."

Some people still think self-talk is corny. However, it's funny because the ones that think it's corny are the ones that haven't even tried it. It's definitely ok to tell yourself the world is yours. Why? Because it is.

Playing it safe is cool until you stuck. People who lack true confidence will play it safe. Average people play it safe. Confident people boss up and go for it. Don't get me wrong, some things like paying your bills, car note/maintenance, rent, mortgage, health, and the person you date shouldn't be taken lightly. Don't just date anybody and get your oil change at the last minute every time. Don't take this out of context. You can most definitely take risk and be smart at the same time.

When I resigned from working for the state, I had about six thousand saved up and all my bills were paid up to date. It only took me a month to get my next job, so once I did, I invested three out of that six thousand on things I need to start my own speaking brand. Without having the amount of confidence I had, none of that would have even happened. And just to be honest, I wouldn't have written this book without having the amount of confidence that I have.

To develop something great, you must be confident. You think when Mark Zuckerberg started the development of Facebook, everybody believed in him? Honestly, it didn't even matter because he was confident enough to go for it anyway. And won, he won BIG! Just imagine if you created one special online social site and a year later your life completely changes. Change is hard to attain without confidence.

When I stopped drinking alcohol, I had to be confident enough to continue to tell individuals I knew, 'no thank you.' if I wasn't confident along my journey of growth, I would have given in and started back drinking and feeling more than just a buzz. Being confidence enables you to take the necessary steps to where you truly want to go in your life. The more steps you successfully take towards greatness, the clearer your vision appears. Clarity brings power. Being confident brings power. If utilized correctly, it will bring you so much power.

Fellas, are you confident enough to tell a beautiful woman, "I'm not interested" because she doesn't value what you value in life. Ladies, are you confident enough to tell a handsome man, "I'm not interested" because he doesn't value what you value out of life. Being Confident increases your focus. It allows you to look at situations from a logical and realistic point of view. Not emotional, please don't make serious life moves off emotions. It's not healthy to move off your feelings because feelings lead to failure. Be confident enough to move off principles. Principles will lead to productivity.

Being confident allows you to invest in your brand or business instead of blowing wads of cash on going out and impressing people that you don't know. Don't think you have to go out all the time because you are in your 20's. Don't think you have to date someone because it'll look better for your social media. Don't think you have to work at the highest paying job you got offered because you think your parents will be happy. Don't think smoking marijuana is cool because it brings you more company. Don't think you have to be the status quo without no true quota.

However, you can go right ahead and let your insecurities show. The more insecurities you have, the more broke you will be. Be confident enough to be different. You don't have to be like everybody else. Whoever told you, you had to, lied right to your face. Be you; that is the only way you will attain self-actualization.

Being unique and different derives from confidence. Confidence isn't something you are born with. Confidence is just like faith; it's something to build. You build confidence through all the experiences, setbacks, failures, achievements, and relationships. If you are serious about growth like I am, your confidence will only get stronger and stronger because the more you improve, the more you will feel good about yourself. You don't have to always feel good to be confident. Just be sure of yourself that everything will fall into place accordingly.

Start today and tell those toxic people in your life that you can't hang out this weekend. Start today and tell those physical attractive individuals that you're not my type because of what you value. Start today and say to your friends around you that I am taking my life to the next level. Start telling your parents today that I don't want to become what you've always wanted me to become. Start today and say to your colleagues that I am chasing my dreams. Telling your spouse today that I'm going to get more out of life, and if you're not trying to go with me, then I'm still going to go. Telling yourself today that you are the most amazing human being that has ever stepped foot on this planet.

Carry out your mission with confidence and don't let anything or anybody stop you from doing so. Boss Up!

PATIENCE

Patience is tricky. And on top of that, it's something I have struggled with for a while in my life, but I think I finally got this thing down. Patience is the ability to wait for something that you desire to get. Patience isn't just waiting itself. I was in school from age 4 to age 25. That's 21 years before I earned my Master's Degree. On top of that, I was in grad school three full years instead of two or one and a half like most people.

But the beautiful thing about patience is that it enables you to stay more focused on your value then the value of an opportunity. As I look at the majority of my peers from high school and undergraduate, I see that many of those individuals rushed something in their life. When you rush something, you decrease the level of value of it.

We desire things that are most valuable to us. This is why when you attain something that you thought was very valuable to you, it didn't really seem as valuable once you actually got it. It actually was valuable, but since you were in a rush to get it, the quality of whatever you got subconsciously decreased.

The harder you work for something, the harder it is to give it up and the more you will cherish it. How do I know this? Because when I was in my phase of dating various women, at one time I tried to get them to open up to me fully, as quickly as possible. Then the crazy thing is once I actually won them over, , in most cases, the desire I once had for the woman changed because it happened too fast So how can we build a true desire for something we are pursuing without changing our drive for it once we actually get what we pursue?

We must be patient. When you wait for something a little longer, it allows you to care more about it. The question is what are you really willing to wait for? What do you truly value?

We will wait for things we value the most. Waiting is a game. Sometimes you wait for something so long and you never get it. Maybe this is why we start to become inpatient along our journey to greatness because we don't want that feeling of disappointment anymore. But with success comes disappointments, plenty of them. You might as well get used to it. It's the wave of life. The catch is to learn from your disappointments as quickly as possible so that next time you will be able to boss up through that thing!

Most people lack patience because they are just not mentally tough enough. Being a mentally tough individual, I have realized that there are a lot of individuals in this world that fear suffering. Why though? Without suffering, we cannot grow. No pain no gain. No struggle no progress. Without patience, we won't reach self-actualization.

Tomorrow isn't promised, so why wait? Why put so much trust into five or ten years from now when everything could end tomorrow? Stop being selfish!!! The reason why you are asking yourself these questions is because you are only thinking about you. Inpatient individuals possess selfish tendencies.

The reason why I think five years, ten years, twenty years down the road is because I want my family to be good, my community, my home church, my people, my country. Just because I may pass in the next couple of years doesn't mean someone I love will.

Have you ever sat down and actually thought about all the people that are depending on you to make it. If you have, it's actually more people than you think or in some cases than you would like. When patience is applied to a skill and authentic individual, it really creates them into a boss. A boss that can't and won't be stopped. Being a boss and reaching self-actualization definitely requires patience. A bunch of it. Yes, some individuals do have breakthroughs in their careers like the Chris Brown's, but just how he didn't expect to blow up so fast, don't you either.

Patience is a virtue and time shouldn't be taken lightly. This means that while you wait for your greatness to manifest into your life, you should be developing your own greatness. Don't just sit around and wait for the opportunity to arrive in your life, prepare for it. You have to focus on the shooting more than the shot. Work while you wait, especially work on yourself and build your value. People wonder why they are getting many opportunities in their field of work, but not growing financially.

You have to practice more than you perform so that when you perform, you do so well that people won't forget about you. Being patient allows you to build a strong foundation. The foundation of your personal growth should not be taken lightly. Your foundation is serious business. If you rush this part of the process, you're pretty much defeating the purpose.

When you know your purpose in life, you become more patient. You know why you are waiting. Without purpose you will be more inpatient and upset because things aren't happening fast enough or how fast you would like it. Just chill my brothers and sisters, your goals will be accomplished, your dreams will be achieved, the life you always wanted to live will happen if you choose to give yourself enough time to develop it. There is something special about an individual who is patient. When a person is patient, it entails that they are in control of themselves; they are not like genuine "so anxious." It's good to be excited and ready, but not anxious. Being anxious leads to anxiety. When anxiety builds, it doesn't feel the best. There will be times where we will be anxious, and it will be very hard to control. This is where growth kicks in. This is the situation where life forces you to sit your butt down and wait. Worst feeling ever, right? When you feel that you are more than prepared for the opportunity and you still haven't got it yet. When you are financially stable to invest in your new business, but you still haven't got the go from the people that you want to be on your team. Life isn't a joke.

Purpose plus patience equals power. So much power. To the best of my knowledge only a few individuals seriously carry out their purpose and have patience doing so, which is why only 1% of individuals in this world reach self-actualization. When waiting for your greatness to develop, you cannot let your emotions get the best of you. I had convinced one of my good friends to invest, the moment he saw his investment went down, he sold his share and got his money back. The crazy thing is, a day later, the amount of the product went back up and surpassed the previous highest amount. He should have just waited, right? But why couldn't he? His emotions got the best of him. Your emotions will make you lose.

I'm telling you from the bottom of my heart, you have to get out of your feelings. Your feelings will allow you to miss out on a lot of great opportunities and in this case financial growth. It's best to take your time with things. Be smooth. Be in control. Be great.

Impatience is a huge reason why most people get out of character throughout their process. One time I helped this guy with a job in which he was making a good 60k salary, bought him a new car, rented him out a new place, and everything was good. Later down the road, he stole funds from the company he was working for. He got greedy. Being greedy comes from the lack of patience. He couldn't just wait for his next commission or regular check to get the funds. He wanted the money right then and there and probably thought he could have gotten away with it. When your emotions get stirred up, you become impatient.

Once again, get out of your feelings. It won't be worth it in the long run. But the question you have to ask yourself is, do you even see yourself still in the race after years and years of chasing your dreams? Are you really about that life? If you want to reach self-actualization, you are probably going to have to be about that life.

"You must be crazy to wait so long for that!" This is something you will hear once you become serious about reaching self-actualization. Things take time and sometimes a lot longer than we ever expected. But that's ok. Don't you quit, you are worth the life you always wanted. Be crazy enough to keep pursuing something when you don't see results right away.

That fast money don't last. Make sure you are gaining and growing solidly and not quicker than a heartbeat. When it took you a while to achieve your goal at hand, you will appreciate it more. You will cherish it more. You will respect it more.

If you don't respect your money, you will spend it all only because you are for sure you are going to get tips the next day.

Having patience teaches us to care about our growth. Have you ever met someone that was doing really good financially, then the next year they are broke? I have. It wasn't me personally, but it was someone I had a tight friendship with at the time. I pray that I never have to experience that. However, these types of things happen because individuals don't respect what they have achieved.

Being patient enables you to sit your but down knowing that you just got paid. It allows you to control your anxiety. It will enable you to understand that credit building is more important than impressing individuals who don't truly care about you.

True growth and development come from respecting the process. The more you respect what you are going after, the more patient you will become with achieving it, and once achieved, the more serious you will be about maintaining it. Being patient along your journey to greatness isn't just about being able to have the patience to withstand all the troubles. It's about being patient enough with yourself when you do get there.

Always know that you are still growing as an individual once you reach a certain level success. People who keep their patient tendencies once their goal is attained exemplify rich mindsets. Be patient. Be rich. You deserve it.

Stop wishing, start working. Faith without work is dead. I have heard people in my church saying, "I'm waiting on God. I'm hoping he comes through." Being patient doesn't mean to do nothing while you are waiting for your blessing. It means having the strength enough to still put forth crazy amounts of effort not knowing when your blessing is going to come. It isn't healthy to try to force life to bless you with things on your time. The world doesn't revolve around you.

The real world will force you to be patient. The moment you think you have everything planned out and structured, something pops up and shifts everything. That's why we have to work for the best and expect the worst along our journey to greatness. I personally expect setbacks and turnarounds to happen from time to time. Having patience when you have a setback enables you to take control of the situation in the best way you can. There is no need to trip when you know this setback is doing nothing but strengthen your patience. When your patience strengthens, everything else about you gets stronger.

Are you patient enough to break your unhealthy habits? Many people never break their unhealthy habits because it takes too long to actually do it. We all know a couple of people that has never changed any of their unhealthy habits. Why? It's because they are emotionally attached to them. There are grown men in their 30s and 40s acting like they are still in their 20s.

I'm pretty sure these men tried to break their unhealthy habits at one point of time in their life, but having enough patience to actually endure the challenges was just too much. Everybody can't handle being patient, not because they don't have the capabilities of doing so, it's because they haven't trained themselves to be patient. True patience is something that is learned. You're not born with it.

If you want to reach self-actualization, you must train yourself to learn patience and not just fake it. Some people will wait only because they know when the prize is coming. That's easy. But waiting for something without knowing when you will actually get it, now that's true Boss stuff right there.

Bosses know how to sit back and wait. Bosses know how to sit there but still while grinding to the top. Bosses know that their time is coming one day, so they won't sweat it nor rush it. Take control of yourself by being patient. Your time is coming, just trust yourself.

Trust enables patience and vice versa. When someone is willing to wait for something special, it presents that they trust that it is going to happen. When people rush and force things, they are not sure of themselves. Or they could just want to hurry it up and get it done. Makes sense, right? But becoming the best version of yourself isn't something you should just want to hurry up and get done. It is something that you want to take your time with. One of my high school football coaches, Mr. Paul Phillips, used to always tell my teammates and I, "Be quick, but don't hurry."

On the football field, he meant to run to the ball but give yourself enough time to read the play. In life, we must run to our dreams, goals, and aspirations, but make sure our vision is clear enough to maintain a sense of direction.

When you're in a hurry, you are all over the place, and your direction isn't on point. Patience brings clarity. Clarity allows you to get something quickly and to be able to know what the heck is going on. Do you truly know what is going on with yourself, your life, your journey?

Think about that for a quick second. There is no need to lie to yourself if you don't. You might need to slow yourself down a little bit and self-reflect about what you really want out of life and measure out to see if the wait will be worth it. I can tell you this; if you are thinking about your dreams on a daily basis, then it is most definitely worth the wait.

Don't get fooled by social media and television. If you are trying to live a life you cannot afford, this will only weaken your patience. It will weaken your patience because you will always try to keep up with the hottest trends and fashions. Then you will wake up one day and realize where you truly are, then be disappointed and continue to live your life impatiently. Don't be weak and give in because the average individuals are doing it. You are not average. You were born great. So, wait for your greatness to be brought out of you. It will be if you just take the time out to manifest it.

You can't expect the average, impatient individuals to rock with you when you take the route of achieving self-fulfillment. They won't understand, and most won't even attempt to gain understanding. Don't waste your time with these individuals. Just like you have trained yourself to be patient, they have trained themselves to be impatient. The behavior is learned. Healthy habits teach you patience and unhealthy habits teach you how to be in a hurry. If you are not teaching yourself how to be patient and even more patient along your process, then you might never get there. However, I know you have what it takes to get there, so just be patient so that you can feel so good about yourself once you reach self-actualization.

Be patient with others as well. Having patience doesn't just mean to be patient with yourself. It also means to be patient with others. Put some trust in others knowing that they will get the job done and provide you with certain opportunities that will take your career, better yet, life to the next level. You can't do it alone. You will need other people to help you along your journey. But you will have to be patient enough to trust that they will come through. Also, patience allows you to understand that others have their own life problems, setbacks, and things to handle.

For instance, if something happened in one of your business partner's life like a loss in the family, the child got sick, or car broke down, you will have to be patient enough to wait for them to come through knowing the deadline wasn't met because of life circumstances. The more you model patience with others, the more they will model patience back with you. It's the law of attraction.

In plain sense, you better not complain about someone's behavior when you are doing the same thing. If someone feels that you trust them in assisting you, then it will increase the chances of them doing so. Now, this doesn't work every time, so don't bet on it. Just know that how you treat people in the means of being patient with them can make a world of difference. We are all placed on this earth to make a difference. And making a difference takes time.

Learn to let others grow on you. Don't expect people to treat you like a God when they first meet you. Even if they have heard great things about you, people are people, and they need time for you to grow on them. Patience not only helps you grow, it helps your friendships, work relationships, business relationships, and love relationships grow. If the people you are consistently hanging around don't respect your process, then they are not being patient with your growth. This is reflection of how they probably feel about themselves as well, so don't take it personal. It's ok. Everybody is entitled to their own opinion and way of thinking. However, if you are serious about reaching self-actualization, you only need to surround yourself around individuals that respect you enough to wait on you to prosper and flourish.

Patience brings peace. Before I became patient, I realized how stressed and worried I was all the time. Even though I was getting things done for some reason, I always wanted my success to come quicker. I was being selfish and impatient. After experiencing certain things in my life, I have become mature and wise enough to know that things don't come when I want them to, things will come when I am ready for them. We attract what we are ready for whether you like it or not. I wouldn't want an opportunity given to me that I wasn't prepared for. Have you ever gotten something you asked for and became overwhelmed with it? I have.

When you are prepared, you can handle and the opportunity. This doesn't mean you won't get frustrated or become worrisome at times; this just means that you can keep your composure. Cool, calm, and collected is how true bosses carry their life. No need to be in a hurry because you know your blessings are coming. Always remember that proper preparation prevents poor performance and poor performance promotes pain.

It's natural to stress, but try not to worry. Be desperate for your dreams, but you don't have to appear desperate for others to provide you with the opportunity you dream of. When people feel like you are constantly rushing your greatness, they may think that you are not in control. Bosses are in control at all times, even when they are doing orders for other people, making others happy, or even making sacrifices for the greater good. Just because you are working for someone or depending on someone to help you start your business or consult your business doesn't mean you are not in control. Being in control means that you are doing everything you can while waiting for your big shot to come. The more you work while you wait, the readier you will be when your big shot comes. This world really does belong to you, but you have to be willing to wait for things to manifest and develop in your own life. Everything takes time, especially your greatness. Boss Up!

CONSISTENCY

Be crazy enough to keep doing it. Be relentless. Average people won't understand you when you do this. They will tell you to "take it easy," "you're doing too much," "give yourself a break." I'm going to tell you this; an average person will never understand a great person. Until the average individual starts moving in the direction of greatness on a serious level, they will be confused about your overdoing of actions. If you want to become the best version of yourself, you can't just do what makes you great sometimes, or every now and then. It takes consistent action.

While in school, I always wrote my essays a little per day, maybe like a page or two. I had some colleagues who would wait until the last week or so and cram it all in. The crazy thing is, in most cases, my grade came out to be higher than my colleagues who waited till the last minutes. On top of that, I kept my peace and sanity. Working on your craft on a day to day basis instead of cramming things in allows you to focus on the details of your craft. Being consistent enables you to pay more attention to what you are doing because you are not in such a rush. If you feel that you are a last-minute person, then it will be difficult reaching self-actualization, not impossible, but difficult because in the real world, you must stay ready. What if you're a parent in a graduate program and you haven't been consistent with writing your term paper and right before it's due your child gets sick? Now you have to take care of your child while they are home from school sick, finish up your term paper, and deal with all the other stressors of life. That would be tough, right? But what if you were consistent enough that you were already done with your paper by the time your child got sick, and you could solely focus on taking care of your child and getting him or her better. You see how life could possibly work if you stay consistent chasing your dreams. Being consistent with pursuing your dreams helps you manage your life better.

Things will happen in your life that will sometimes force you to pay attention to something else besides your dreams and goals. And if you haven't been constantly pounding at your goals when you had the time to, now you are even more behind. That may even stress you out more. Consistency can bring your harmony. Aren't you tired of being stressed?

Consistency doesn't necessarily speed up the process, but it can help you gain confidence about what you are doing. If Steph Curry didn't shoot so many shots in practice, would he be confident enough to shoot nearly half court shots in a real game and bank it. No, I don't think so. The more you do something, the more you will develop your groove of doing it, the more you will understand what works for you and what doesn't. Being consistent will help you learn you more. You are worth the investment.

I remember when I used to host events with my New Elite Brothers, we were so consistent with getting people the information to our party. We put flyers in every gas station, liquor store around town and surrounding towns. We were completely relentless on social media, we did not stop posting about our party. I literally got blocked by others on Twitter on multiple occasions because I kept posting about our event so much. And this still didn't stop me. I promoted our event like my life depended on it. People thought I was crazy. I was. I was crazy enough to shoot for the results I wanted. My New Elite brothers and I actually got results at our events. We packed out the place, people stated that they enjoyed the party afterward, and we gained quality compensation for our events.

Our goal was to achieve the real reasons for throwing a college party, which were packing out the venue, making sure the people who attended had a lifetime experience, and financial gain. We weren't playing any games. Also, we threw an event every semester to keep our buzz going. People will eventually respect your consistency once they can feel you are not going to stop pursuing your goals anytime soon. Being consistent breeds seriousness. Do what you love enjoyably, but make sure you are serious about it and others can feel that you are serious. Others will support you more when you become relentless in carrying out your mission. Consistency will bring you a crowd. Leaders are consistent. You know you are a leader, so be one and stop playing around.

Consistency breaks down fear. The reason why consistency breaks down fear is because consistency builds confidence and confidence is the opposite of fear. This is time to start attacking your fears over and over and over again. This will make you a more powerful individual. If you are not consistent in attacking your fears, feeling good about overcoming them will be off and on. You don't truly want to be fearful. You know you deserve to feel good about what you do. Boss up and keep doing it. Scared money doesn't make no money.

Consistency is key. People say this all the time, what does the key of consistency actually lead to? Sometimes people do something all the time, and nothing changes in their life. Consistency is only key if you are doing the right thing over and over again. The right thing for your mental growth, emotional growth, spiritual growth, financial growth, and physical growth. Now if you are consistently shopping and going on vacations, then are you really trying to build your credit score? Probably not, especially if your income doesn't support your spending.

Now if you are consistently putting money back into your savings, making smart investments, and paying your credit debt off, then that would be key. Some of us are consistent in doing the wrong things, and that's why we don't grow. Consistency is only helpful to your success if you are doing the right thing for your success.

Consistency will build habits. The more often you wake up early, the more often you respond to all your emails every day, the more often you say good morning to your spouse, the more often you work out your body, and the more often you don't respond to someone else's negativity, the more you will build a habit of doing so. Once something is a habit, it becomes emotionally attached to us. This means that we start doing it subconsciously and we don't need anyone to remind us of doing it. It becomes a part of us. Make sure the healthy things you do are your true habits and not the unhealthy things. The more positive and effective habits you possess on your journey to success, the more likely you will reach self-actualization. Be consistent about your growth and the growth of others around you.

The more often you do what you have to do the more likely you'll be able to live how you want to live one day. Remember, when being consistent be patient and have faith. If you know that what you are doing is working and helping you get one step closer to the promise land, then you must trust yourself to keep doing it even when times get hard.

What you repeatedly do will become who you are. If you work out every morning to start your day and eat a decent breakfast, then you could be perceived as a healthy person. We have to always remember that our perception is our reality. What you do over and over again will become attached to who you are. And yes, some of us do have some unhealthy habits. We do have some things that aren't so good consistently.

That's why I said earlier in this book at it's not just about your consistency itself, it is also about what you actually do consistently. If you have a son or daughter and they seem to always get in fights at school, and you keep telling them "stop fighting" or "don't do that anymore," then does that really work? It all depends. But from what I have seen from working with at-risk youth is that they have to practice walking away from the fight. In order to become consistent at anything, you must get started doing it! Once the at-risk youth actually controls his or her aggression and walks away from the fight, then we have progress. And the more they walk away from fights, the more they are likely to walk away again.

Your consistency in what you do builds who you are as a person. If you want to become the person who have always desired to be, make sure your habits are in alignment with that person.

Why do the wealthy keep getting wealthier and the poor gets poorer? It is because of what they consistently do. It's really simple. Wealthy people have wealthy habits, and poor people have poor habits. Now, this doesn't mean you are a bad person because you're poor. You are still a great person. This just means that you are not doing what the wealthy people do. Your habits and routine aren't similar to a wealthy person. That's it. I believe one of the quickest ways for a poor person to turn his or her life around and reach self-actualization is to change some of their habits. They must change what they consistently do. Changing your routine to something completely different will feel very uncomfortable at first, and you might want to change your mind. However, let's get off feelings and get on principles.

There is greatness all inside of you, but you can't be off and on, wish-washy or shaky about it. You must be firm and diligent about you becoming the person you truly want to become. The process you are experiencing right now is molding you to become the person you dreamed of. However, we must be consistent with our actions in doing so. If we continue to build the habits that are necessary to our success, then we are strengthening our faith, trust, and commitment to it.

Once you become faithful over few, you will become ruler over all. Even when I am feeling under the weather, I still make sure I go to the gym. Now, my workout maybe lighter and shorter, but at least I'm still going. The strongest individuals you will ever meet will be the ones who work hard even when they don't feel well. The more consistent you are at doing this, the more you are ready to take your life to the next level.

Stretch yourself. Keep practicing those healthy habits. Practice doesn't always make perfect, but after thousands and thousands of hours of beating on your craft, it can definitely become permanent.

When is enough, enough? When do we stop being consistent in pursuing our purpose in life? Well, the answer to your question is never. You should never stop going after what you truly want to become. Your life is worth the investment. You just have to make the investment. You are already the person you want to become, you just have to bring it out of you.

Consistency doesn't necessarily mean insanity. It means putting positive energy and focus towards something that will help you reach prosperity. For example, insanity would be if I went to the gym and did the same workout every time I went, but consistency can be described as me just going to the gym a lot. Being consistent doesn't mean to get comfortable in what you are doing to reach self-actualization because you do it so much. It means to adjust what you are doing, but with the same purpose for doing so. It means to keep acting towards your mission in life literally non-stop and making those specific adjustments along the way to your greatness. Remember, consistency is only effective if what we do is what is needed to be done to achieve our goals at hand. I remember when I used to be a consistent drinker, yes every day, for at least 3 years straight. I became such a consistent drinker that my body became obsessed with it, and I became emotionally invested in it.

Now that I no longer drink, glory be to God, I have replaced that unhealthy habit with speaking. The reason why I enjoy speaking so much and I am so consistent with it because it allows me to cope with life stressors. Yes, I do stress too, I am not perfect. The more I speak, the more I feel better about my life. I have a built a strong attachment with speaking and serving others because those two things make me feel so good about myself. Just make sure the habits you are building are habits you can keep building and not habits that can take your life or that one day you will eventually have to stop because of health or financial problems.

If your consistency is bringing boredom, then you are not obsessed enough with your journey; your journey to self-actualization that is. The reason why you should be doing whatever you do all the time is because you are in love with your purpose, you are in love with your mission, and most of all, you are in love with your process. If you haven't fallen in love with your craft, then you are not ready to perfect it yet. And I know sometimes we are not ready and that is ok. But just know there is another individual out there who is busting their bottom and going full force at the same thing you are trying to achieve. We have to remember always, the way you view consistency may not be how someone else view consistency. We cannot limit our own greatness to the environment we live in or the group of individuals we hang with the most. For example, you may view consistency by grinding 40 hours a week at whatever you do, and I may see it grinding it 65-75 hours a week at what I do.

You may consider working out 2-3 days a week as being consistent, and I may consider working out 5-6 days a week. So, our own perception of consistency is important because people grow and prosper at the rate that is best for them. However, just be mindful if someone is getting better results than you are because this could be an indication that they are working on their craft more than you are.

Be a freak of nature. Do something so much where it doesn't even make you tired anymore. Go after your dreams so relentlessly that people will block you on social media. This actually happened to me when I kept sending my friends motivational videos through direct messages. People eventually got tired of it and became annoyed by the crazy pursuit of my purpose. But you know what, that's ok, I can take some hate, I can take a lot of it actually. If you haven't developed any haters because of how much you work towards your aspirations, then you must not be consistent enough in doing so.

When people began to verbalize that you work too much towards achieving your dreams and you start getting the results you have always envisioned, then you will know that you are consistent enough. If you are not there yet, just keep doing it. And one day your day will come, but you have to trust that it will. Boss Up!

PERSEVERANCE

When your body tells you to give up, but your mind and soul tells you to keep pushing. Having the tenacity to continue to do something with delayed gratification can be mind-throbbing and make you feel all types of ways inside. However, the beauty of becoming a true boss is having the will to do what others won't do. Bosses are just different from your everyday normal person. They just move differently.

I remember when I was studying for the Masters Social Work Licensing exam in 2016 right after I achieved my master's degree. And I was so focused and determined to pass the exam the first time around, but not to know that I didn't really have the right study information. The first time I took the exam in July 2016, I failed it by 21 questions. Bummer right? My heart was beating out my chest the entire test. I really felt like my life was on the line. So I got my first job working for the state in August 2016, and of course, it felt good to put some money in my pocket, I'm not going to lie. So once I got the hang of my kind of job, I began studying for the licensing exam again. This was around the end of October. Also, I had registered for Dr. Cobb two-day licensing exam prep-class at the University of Texas at Arlington which was scheduled to be on November 17th and 18th.

Then I had scheduled to take my exam the following Monday on Nov. 21st, 2016. Perfect move, right? Yea, I thought so too. Not knowing that the evening of Nov. 21st, 2016 was going to give me one of the craziest feelings of my life. Nope, I didn't past the exam. This time I failed by two freaking points. I was so hurt. When I found out I only failed by two questions, I smashed my hand down on the counter, kicked two or three chairs, and said a numerous amount of curse words.

After paying $250 for the prep class and repaying $230 to retake the licensing exam, I still failed. In total, I had already spent nearly a thousand dollars for this exam. That night didn't go so well. I didn't want to talk to anybody and I got drunk, so drunk. Still wondering where the perseverance comes in, right?

Baby, give me one more chance. As the months went by and the year of 2017 came, I truly felt that I was ready to give the licensing exam one more shot. In the state of Texas, you are only able to take any social work licensing exams up to three times. What most individuals don't know is that the licensing exam test changes every time you take it, so you never really know which version you are getting. I began studying again around the end of January. This time I had all the information, study guides, webinars, and mutual support. I just knew in March of 2017 I was going to smash this test! I took the test in the morning this time because I'm naturally a morning person.

I prayed in the car and smoked a black and mild in the car to keep calm. Yea I know, crazy combination right? But it's what I had to do to calm my nerves because my heart was close to popping out of my chest. I went in that building with all confidence telling myself this is MY time. For some reason, this test didn't have some information that I had studied for, and I was confused. About halfway throughout the test, I knew this was going to be a close one. I had forgotten the test was 170 questions because they only score 150 questions, and the other 20 aren't scored at random. So about the last hour of the test, I thought I had 30 more questions left, then I remembered it was actually 170 questions in total. My heart started racing because I had to answer 50 questions in an hour. To be honest, the last 20 questions I just picked an answer. On the screen again, it said I failed. I failed once again! I went to the lobby and came to found out that I failed by only 5 questions.

This had me furious for a second, then I told myself, "Really Bryan, are you really going to let this test define your success and who you are as a person?" I was chasing the status of becoming an LMSW. When I look back at this story, it makes me laugh, but I never passed the Masters Social Work licensing exam, so what did I achieve? Nothing, right? In this case, it wasn't what I achieved, it was who I became. I have never invested so much time, energy, and money in a test like that ever in my life. This experience made me more of a monster. Even though I failed all three times, I still felt unstoppable. I just knew by me failing all three times, a blessing from God was coming down to rain on me soon.

I talked to my mother about not passing the licensing exam, and she told me, "Maybe God has something better in store for you." I told my mom, "I believe so too." In the beginning of April, some things weren't going well at my job and I started to feel like the environment I was in was changing my character for the worse. I had become judgmental, always rushing from place to place, and started to look down on others. The job I had at the time didn't make me feel like I was really empowering others. It felt more like I was working for a social correction than a social service. I started to apply for other job openings every single night and scheduling interviews. I put my two weeks-notice in on April 17, 2017. Once I gave my notice to my supervisor, it was such a relief. That Friday prior to the 14th, I posted my first motivational video on YouTube. I began posting some of my older videos from my phone onto my YouTube channel as well. On May 1st, I officially left working for the state. Even though I had no job secured, I still felt like I had achieved something. After failing the licensing exam three times and failing at my job, I started to find myself truly. After all that I persevered through, I began to find me, after 26 years of living, I began to realize why I was really placed on this earth. I knew my purpose was to empower others through my speaking, coaching, educating, guiding, and mentoring.

All the detours and roadblocks led me to creating my speaking brand "Bryan Humphrey Speaks." By the middle of May, I had seriously cut down on my alcohol intake as well. And just two months after I left working for the state, I gave up drinking alcohol completely. I gave up being a player. I started to find peace within myself.

On June 1st, I started my new job working in the field of behavioral health. My new job allowed me to have a flexible schedule. I could work any day of the week and majority of the day. Once I started to actually perform my job duties, I felt as if this is what I should have been doing.

My new job, my speaking brand, and my life all were aligning in my true purpose and vision. Sober life was actually pretty good too. So just think about it. Sometimes in life, we must go through all the nonsense and chaos just to achieve ourselves, to achieve true success. And sometimes the things that we are pursuing may not be what God really has in store for us all along. This was definitely an example of delayed gratification.

You may be trying to seek gratification in the wrong thing, maybe that's why you haven't achieved it yet. Don't ever question life or God why something is the way it is. We have to trust ourselves along our journey to greatness and know that everything that happens to us is never against us. It's for us. The things we go through, good or bad, are molding us to become the person we always have to be, but only if we choose to learn from our experiences and not dwell on them. In order to persevere in life, you can't dwell on the problem. You must go forth and seek the solution.

Rich people focus on solving the problem, and poor people focus on the problem itself. And you are not poor; you are chosen, you are valued, you are special, you are cherished, and you are amazing!

Just keep fighting. Once you make it up in your mind that you have no choice but to make it, then you will do whatever it takes to get there. Perseverance in lamest terms means changing your wants to a must. You must graduate college. You must workout consistently. You must have a successful business. You must have a wonderful family. You must be top salesman for the company you work for. You must become a professional athlete. Yes! The pressure is on.

However, diamonds are made under pressure. You're definitely not an octagon or hexagon, so fight through those hard times and keep coming back like your life absolutely depended on it. An individual who perseveres consistently is dangerous. This individual can't be stopped. This individual has a relentless work ethic. This individual can't be ignored because their strength goes unnoticed. When the purpose of what you do becomes more important than what you do, you will develop tough skin.

Even when people tell you no, reject you, curse you out, tell you to get out of their office and stop blowing up their phones, you still boss up and do it anyway. If you are going to be a boss, you have to really be one. This is not a game. This is real life and if you don't boss up and persevere, life will put you on your bottom like you were never here on this earth in the first place. Stop giving up because someone told you it couldn't be done. You can do it. You are already the person you want to become, you just have to bring it out of you.

When life gets hard, go harder. Success and achieving greatness isn't that deep. The moment you give up on your dreams is the moment you give up on yourself. You are the dream and nothing less. In life, there will be hard times, and sometimes they are so hard we don't know what to do. This is where faith comes in. Perseverance is only carried out on a serious basis with faith. Faith without work is dead. Believing in what you are pursuing should be a number one priority. You think I would keep chasing my own dreams if didn't believe it will happen? How you view what you do will determine how serious you are while doing.

Are you a salesman that goes to individuals thinking this person isn't interested in my product or are you the salesman that thinks, I will make this person interested in my product because of who I am? The mindset is just different. Your mindset will depict your reality. Being negative will get you negative results. However, once you develop the thought process to see the positive out of every situation, that's when bosses are created! A boss can see the positive out of every situation. It doesn't matter how dark the road is that you are traveling, when you can see that glimpse of light, then you won't stop no matter what.

Be tenacious and stop budging. When I first gave up drinking alcohol, I had a couple of individuals told me, "Bryan, just take a shot with me, let's drink a beer together. It won't hurt." They also told me, "I promise I won't say anything; this will just be between you and me." I looked at them dead in their eye and told them, "No thank you. I'm good." Be strong-willed enough to say no when the offer seems convincing.

When you are on the way to reaching self-actualization, some people will purposely try to knock you off your game, especially the individuals that know your weaknesses. It's crazy because sometimes the people close to you will be the same ones who try to get you to budge. "Just drink Bryan," "Just be normal for a day," "Let's go splurge at the strip club," "Take off and let's go on a random vacation," "Stop being so uptight and relax," "Just hit the blunt once with us," "Ride out with your boys man, we boys stop tripping."

The truth of the matter is, once you start to become stretched and people can see that you are headed to the top, they will begin to feel just a little uncomfortable. So, they will ask you to do things to make them feel more comfortable when you are around them. This is the time to persevere so much that even people who are close to you sometimes feel uncomfortable around you. This is the time to stop playing games and be a boss baby! Let's go!

I appreciate the things that are hard because the things that are hard are the things that make me. Things like: having redo a year of grad school, stop drinking alcohol, create my own brand from scratch, working out 5-6 days a week, quitting my job working for the state without no job secured, speaking to over 200 high school graduating seniors my first speaking gig ever, cutting off old friends, and not going out as much. Yes, there is more, but that would take me all day to write.

What makes me keep going even in the face of difficulty? You, yes, you guys. Knowing that I have people looking up to me and putting their trust in me my character has to be on point at all times. I can't budge because we are homies. This is my reputation on the line. I can't afford to lose all the individual's trust that I have gained throughout my life just for about 30 minutes of wasted pleasure. My life is too pleasurable; it is pleasurable because I am constantly improving. I just love improvement. I truly believe that true happiness and fulfillment come from progress.

In order to attain true happiness and fulfillment, we must persevere through those tough times. We must say yes even when our body says no . We must keep coming back even when there is no instant gratification. We must, we must.

Look in the mirror; there is something strong that you will see. A king, a queen, and as Bob Proctor always states, "You are God's highest form of creation." We, as human beings, were already built to be tough and steadfast. The more you see the worth in you, the more you will be able to persevere. Even in the times when you feel like nobody has your back, literally, you still go for your goals and dreams anyway. Now that's some real Boss stuff. I have to always keep in mind that my dream belongs to me and I can't expect someone to work as hard as me for what I want.

However, as humans, we are naturally attracted to individuals who persevere. Being around someone who doesn't give up makes yourself feel stronger. When you persevere along your journey to reaching self-actualization, you will weed out the individuals that were in your life for the wrong reason. If you stay strong and don't let others get the best of you, you will know who really has your back.

Keep this in mind; only few individuals will really have your back. My step-dad, Mr. Donald Wesson, always told my brothers and I that, "You will only have two or three real friends, if you can get a handful of five people, then you are one lucky and blessed son of a gun." I never really understood this statement until I started truly going after what I desired for my life. Once you become serious about what you want for yourself, people start to become shaky. I've never been one of those shaky and wish-washy individuals when it comes to friendships, so I couldn't tell you how to be shaky. But I can tell you for sure if you want to get to the top you must keep on going chasing your greatness even if the people around you aren't really about that life. perseverance is all about that action.

Are you willing to continue to do what you are doing even if you will lose your approval of others? Are you willing to keep on when people call you a sell-out, trader, and even too good for them? Now let's be honest, if that's how they feel then I understand, but one thing about a boss is that he "can't stop, won't stop" -P-Diddy.

Here are some steps that could help you
persevere in life more often:

- Break your unhealthy habits.

- Cut off individuals who drain you emotionally if you're able to.

- Avoid environments that will make you become weak until you are strong enough to handle it.

- Set deadlines. Have an idea in your head when you want the goal you're pursuing to be achieved.

- Have thick skin. Don't take everything so personal. Most people won't believe in you until you actually make it.

- Embrace your haters. Your haters want you to budge so that you can stop being so dang great. When you can embrace your haters, you allow their negative energy to fuel your fire and make you press on even harder.

- Take care of yourself. Make sure you do the things that help you deal with your life. I work out, pray, read, listen to smooth jazz, sleep six hours a day, set personal boundaries, self-reflect 30 minutes a day every day, and create my to-do list at the beginning of every week.

- Learn to say no. Be strong enough to tell people no, sometimes even the ones you love. This will help you stay grounded. Building a habit of meaning what you say will help you persevere so much.

- Get around individuals that are actually doing what you want to do. This will open your eyes to realize that what you are going for is possible, better yet worth it.

- Let the word "no" make you smile. The word no only means that a better yes is coming sooner or later. Don't worry my brothers and sisters.

- Take time for yourself. Learn who you are and stop living for somebody else. It's easy for a pretender to give up because they are not being true. However, when you are true to self and know what you want out of life, you will be very difficult to stop.

- Get on principles. Being aware of how you feel is great, but acting in your feelings can lead to destruction. If you don' have a list of principles you live by, now is the time to. You can either create your own principles or you can follow a trusted list of ones. I follow the ten commandments.

- Get around positive people, listen to positive audio tapes, and watch positive videos. The more positive you are about your journey to greatness, the more you will be able to embrace the harsh reality of it.

We all have the right to be a boss and to reach self-actualization. However, we must be willing to do whatever it takes to make it happen. Staying focused and disciplined is one of the most important things to achieving true success. Becoming the best version of you isn't some easy route. It will be a challenge to press on when times are rough, but I know you can do it. Boss Up!

COMPETITIVENESS

Being competitive doesn't mean to compare. It just entails the concept of stepping your game up. Reaching self-actualization takes one knowing that he or she isn't the only one pursuing the same dream. When we were young and in elementary school, the person who didn't place got rewarded a green ribbon for participating in the event. Now, for children , that's totally acceptable; however, when I got to high school, things got more serious. It wasn't just if you try you would be fine.

In high school sports, from my experience, there was no green participation ribbon, participation trophy or even consistent acknowledgment from your coaches when you just participated. It was about getting the job done, it was about placing in the event, it was about getting better, and overall it was about doing whatever it took to beat your opponent. Winners never quit, and quitters never win. I learned this quote in 1st grade. However, every single day of my life, especially when things get difficult, I tell myself this.

If you quit whatever you are doing, it is impossible for you to win. Don't quit on your dreams and goals. Don't quit on your journey towards greatness. Don't quit on making this world a better place. Don't quit on financial freedom. Don't quit on your family, friends. And most of all, don't quit on you. You are most definitely worth the light at the end of the tunnel. As a matter of fact, the light is already inside of you, you just have to bring it out.

I have always been competitive by nature. I have always been an extrovert type of person. I loved to be challenged. The thrill of somebody else's performance making me want to do better is something so beautiful. Now, I realize that everybody isn't competitive, and some individuals like to move at their own pace, which is totally fine. We are supposed to move at our own pace, but that doesn't mean we have to be blind to everyone that is going for exactly what we are going for. You are not, and you will never be the only person trying to grow in your field of work. It doesn't matter how unique and specific your field of work is, there will always be some competition.

Now, we don't have to view it as competition, and that's understandable. But once you become self-aware of who you are and what it takes to really live out your mission, you know it will take a certain level of skill to reach self-actualization. Self-actualization isn't given to anyone. Self-actualization is earned. Respect is earned. Your income is earned. If you are a speaker like myself, we have to realize that the top speakers have a certain level of skill as a speaker. Speaking is a craft and an art. And if you aren't self-aware enough to be competitive, you will get overlooked. True competitors are hungry and honest individuals. A true competitor keeps coming back, may talk some smack, has tough skin, and will do whatever it takes to be the winner. Reaching greatness starts with wanting to outdo others indirectly or directly.

Don't be outworked. Whether you are in sales, private practice, education, sports, acting, or even an Instagram sensation. You think you are the only one doing what are you doing? No, not at all. So why not be competitive? Why not wake up earlier? Why not stay up later? Why not put more groundwork in? Why not? If we as human beings know we live in a dog eat dog world, why can't we all be competitive monsters. Everybody isn't wired for greatness. However, anybody can become wired if they choose to.

Your life outcomes will be depicted from what you actually want and what you feel that you deserve. Competitive individuals want more by nature. I think it's good to have that dog in you to want to supersede others. If an individual has settled with where they are at, then that is totally fine. However, if self-actualization isn't reached, you won't have true freedom. True freedom comes from reaching self-actualization.

I do truly believe that only 1-2% of individuals on this earth are actually free. They are free financially, spiritually, emotionally, physically, and mentally. Freedom is earned. How can we become more competitive to earn freedom in our own lives? Well first, we must know why we are competing, how we are doing so, and what we are competing for. I don't know about you guys reading this great book, but I am competing for freedom. I don't want to live life feeling confined to someone else's standards of living. I want to be able to create my own standards for my own life.

When it comes to taking ownership of your life, being a competitive freak of nature will get you there so much quicker, I believe. The phenomenal actor Will Smith once stated, "The only thing that I see that is distinctly different about me is I'm not afraid to die on a treadmill. I will not be out-worked, period. You might have more talent than me, you might be smarter than me, you might be sexier than me, you might be all of those things you got it on me in nine categories. But if we get on the treadmill together, there are two things: you're getting off first, or I'm going to die. It's really that simple, right?

You're not going to out-work me. It's such a simple, basic concept. The guy who is willing to hustle the most is going to be the guy that just gets that loose ball. The majority of people who aren't getting the places they want or aren't achieving the things that they want in this business is strictly based on hustle. It's strictly based on being out-worked; it's strictly based on missing crucial opportunities. I say all the time, if you stay ready, you ain't gotta get ready."

This quote by Mr. Will Smith hit home for me and I hope it hit home for you as well. Are you willing to die for what you are going for? True competitors don't live in fear or doubt. I'm not saying that I haven't felt those feelings before, but a true competitor has relentless work ethic and will not stop.

A true competitor will sometimes annoy others, especially when others are not a true competitor. Don't take it personal when someone doesn't understand your drive to do something. We have to remember that everyone isn't wired to be boss. Even though anyone has the capability of being a boss once they start thinking like one. Bosses are competitive and there is no way around it. competitiveness starts with self-awareness. It starts with knowing what it's going to take for you to outwork others consistently to get to the top and for you to work even harder to stay up there.

Stay around others who challenge you to do better. Being competitive starts with your immediate circle of friends. If you are around people that you know you outwork and are a lot farther along your journey to greatness, then it's time to find some new friends buddy. Now, sometimes to become more competitive we must change our lifestyle and break those unhealthy habits. When you are around someone that is performing much better than you at what you are doing, we must realize that this person's lifestyle has to be different. Being competitive doesn't always entail just working harder to master the skill at hand. It's also working harder on self. When an individual becomes more valuable as a person because of how they live their lives, it will change the whole ball game.

For example, just speaking from personal experience, once I stopped drinking alcohol, it allowed me to wake up earlier, go to bed at my set bedtime, stop hanging around certain people that weren't adding value to my life, and become stronger spiritually. Now for those reading this book who drink alcohol, I am not trying to downplay you guys. You may not have a drinking issue, and you may be doing perfectly fine. However, for myself quitting drinking alcohol, it has been a definite game changer for me. I was more than a social drinker, I was a serious drinker. I drank every day for three years straight. I didn't need an event or legit reason to drink, I just did for the heck of it, and it was how I coped with life.

But how does all of this tie into being competitive? Well, let me break it down. I truly believe most individuals don't reach self-actualization because they have one or two unhealthy habits that they must break before they have their breakthrough. Some of the habits we have are holding us back from putting forth the effort towards our goals and dreams as we would like. I can't tell you what your unhealthy habits are because that isn't my lane to do so. However, here is a list of some unhealthy habits that could possibly hold you back from being the competitor that you want to be:

- **Lying to self.** This is the first one listed for a reason. In order to become more competitive, you must become more self-aware. To become more self-aware, you have to become honest with yourself.

- **Sleeping in.** I understand everybody isn't a morning person, but if woke up just one or two hours earlier than when you normally do, it would make a world of difference.

- **Smoking too much marijuana or indulging in more serious drugs.** (I don't condone anyone to use drugs, but you know deep down inside when you are investing too much time and energy into it.)

- **Drinking too much alcohol.**
  (just like drugs, you know your limits.)

- **Procrastinating.** Stop worrying so much and go after what you deserve. If you are trying to compete better in a financial sense, just remember, scared money don't make no money.

- **Not working out or working out inconsistently.**
  Working your body out consistently scientifically gives you more energy throughout the day to get more things done.

- **Lack of organization and structure.** Start writing down the things you need to get done every day, have desired time you want to get out of bed, and set deadlines.

- **Going out clubbing or bar hopping every weekend.**
  This is big one because working on the weekends consistently will take you from good to great. If you want to be more competitive, put in more work. it's simple.

- **Going out on dates every single week.** There is nothing wrong with dating, but casual dating is played out and it will slow you down from your greatness. Only go out on dates with individuals you feel can add value to your life. It's always good to get to know a person some through text messaging, direct messaging on social media, or even on a phone call before taking them out. This is why I love exchanging social media information so I can get a glimpse of the person's lifestyle and interest Yes, we all get lonely at times, but please don't go out on dates just for company. Date with a purpose.

- **Hanging out with people who don't challenge you.** Now I get it, we have friends that we have been cool with for a long time, and we want to catch up with those individuals and that is perfectly fine. However, in this case, I am talking about your inner circle, not necessarily your co-workers, but the people that know you for you. If you are trying to become competitive and nobody around you is pushing you to become better, now that is a problem. Our environment plays a big part in how competitive we will be.

Is there such thing as being overly competitive or too competitive? This question really all depends on what you are aiming for. Someone may call you an overachiever and deep down inside you feel like you haven't achieved enough. Success is how we view our goals. So no, I personally don't believe anybody can be too competitive or over competitive.

If you want to achieve greatness, then boss up and go get it. I'm not mad at you. You go ahead with your bad self. If one wants to reach self-actualization and compete with the top dogs, then he or she must set very high goals. Being one of the best at what you do is very intentional and deliberate. Success isn't achieved on accident. Greatness doesn't happen by mistake. Self-actualization isn't reached by coincidence. Becoming a true boss is only accomplished from being competitive enough to do whatever it takes to get there. I say this once again; true bosses are competitive.

We have to stay hungry, like literally. Slow feet don't eat, so go and get it. Be crazy and competitive enough to outdo everybody else's expectations of you, then set higher ones for yourself. I know this may sound crazy to you, but if you do this, you will be in that one to two percent of individuals that actually reach true freedom. Compete for your freedom because your freedom is most definitely worth it.

Compete hard, very hard. You may not win every battle, but if you hate losing like I do, then I know you are definitely not trying to lose. Let's be real, losing sucks man. It really does. However, losing is never a loss, it's only lesson. Each loss you experience should teach you something new. If every loss you experience is not teaching you something new, then it's time to compete harder. That means it's time to put in more work towards becoming the person you've always wanted to become. Competing hard doesn't mean to just work on your craft, it also means to work on you. The better and healthier you are, the more you will enable yourself for growth. Competition is about growth and outworking others.

The more you grow on the inside, and the more you produce on the outside, the higher you will go up on the totem pole. We have to remember it's harder to stay the top of the totem pole once we get there. So now we must become even more competitive. Being competitive is a habit amongst the great people. Why do you think great people just keep getting better in life? Once you become emotionally invested in being a competitor, it's hard to stop. It's really hard to stop. I love competition, over the years I have developed a habit to not only be competitive with others but within myself as well. I consistently ask myself what I can do to become a better person. If you want different results, you must become different. True change comes from the inside out. I challenge you, yes you reading this book to compete for change within you, to compete with self, to compete to become the you that you have always wanted to become. You deserve your freedom. You deserve to reach self-actualization.

Don't be afraid to outdo others, shoot, why not be great? Life isn't about sitting around and being stagnant. Life is about growth, it's about prosperity and it's about purpose. The purpose of what you do is more important than what you do. Your purpose derives from your why. And if your why is strong enough, you will never stop competing. I believe that competition makes this world a better place. It brings the best out of us. Some may say the United States of America marketplace is too competitive, but maybe it's just time to set higher goals.

We do live a very competitive country in comparison to other countries all across the world. Some may say we live in a greedy country because the United States of America is the richest place on the world. "Life will force you to boss up" -Mr. Ricquan Williams. This world isn't a joke. I'm not going to lie. It can actually be pretty harsh at times. This is why being competitive is crucial to self-fulfillment and freedom. Life is beautiful. Life is a struggle. Life is a beautiful struggle.

Put your foot down and keep going. You don't have to feel sorry for being so competitive. The world belongs to you. If nobody has ever told you, "You're too much competition" that means it's time to become more competitive. The greats love competition. They dwell on it. Is it true to say that the greats are just simply crazy and psycho? Well, that could be true to a certain extent, but I would just say the greats just love to be challenged. Instead of bagging away from competition they embrace it. For instance, if someone who is a veteran at what he is doing, then some young guy comes along and starts getting some shine, the veteran welcomes the youngster. There is no need to become jealous and/or spiteful because someone half your age performs just as well as you do. The youngster could have started at such an early age. There are teenagers getting college degrees now. There are eight and nine-year-old CEO's. That's just life. Life is a serious business and it's time to put your best foot forward and reach self-actualization.

Living a life of fulfillment and richness isn't impossible. Not at all. You just have to want it for yourself and your family. The crazy thing about life is that you have to really compete for your freedom. I keep repeating this because it is important. This real world isn't going to spoon feed you on a silver plate. The wealthiest or the top 1% financially able individuals in our great country of the United

States of America own one third of all the money. Sounds crazy right? But it's true. I have heard some people say, "This country is unfair," "rich people are greedy," "people who have kids late are selfish," "people who wait to seriously date only care about themselves," "you are dumb for leaving corporate America," and all types of others things. If you have mentioned anyone of these statements ever before, it only entails that you are not competing hard enough for your own personal freedom.

Sometimes we think it's right to assume things about the individual that is doing so well and why they are doing so well when in reality we should be asking that individual what makes you do so well and how? Let's appreciate the individuals that are extremely competitive, especially if you're not their current competition. "If you can't beat them join them."

I thrive off others positive and prosperous energy. Yes, I believe I am most definitely an extrovert. I love competition. Even though I carry myself cool, calm, and collected, I am addicted to competition. I don't think it's nothing wrong with always wanting to improve at what you do every day. But not only that, most importantly, I believe it's absolutely nothing wrong with wanting to improve who you are as a person.

What is the one or two things that is holding you back from being more competitive? Mine was my drinking problem and my player ways with women. I no longer drink alcohol, and I am completely upfront and genuine with every woman I meet. Breaking these two unhealthy habits have enhanced my focus tremendously, which has allowed me to become more competitive in life point blank period. Compete harder. Boss Up!

APPRECIATION

Being great starts with being grateful. We have to always remember everything that happens to us in our lives is for us and never against us. There is a positive and something to gain out of every situation we experience, yes even the harsh ones. I understand that life can be so crazy at times with it's disappointments and let downs, but that's ok, well at least for me. I am thankful for every single experience in my life. I don't view my losses as losses, I view them as lessons. Sometimes we should just say "thank you for being you" to someone we love and care about. It seems we say thank you more for what someone has done instead of just thanking individuals for being themselves. On our journey to greatness, a lot of things will happen, good and bad. However, everything that happens to us is only to mold us to become the individual we need to become to attain the goals and dreams we set.

Express your appreciation not only through verbiage, but through action. Here is a list of things you can do below:

- **Keep your promises.** Always do what you told someone that you were going to do for them.

- **Be prompt.** Being on time to events, work, meetings, dates, etc., shows that you appreciate the opportunity you are given.

- **Do more than required.** One things I hear very successful people say all the time is, do more than what you are paid for.

- **Give back.** Whether it's donating to a non-profit, feeding the homeless, or throwing a fun event for the youth, all this shows that we care. Grateful people care and give back.

- **Stay consistent and down even when times get tough**. This is a difficult one to actually carry out, but if done will leads to a huge victory in the long run.

- **Practice on your craft**. You may be great at what you do. You could even be really great. However, when you are thankful for your gift, you continuously work on it regardless of how much you have accomplished from it.

- **Take care of self**. Taking care of yourself entails that you are thankful for life itself and that you don't take it for granted. We have to remember, the better you can take care of you, the better you will be capable of taking care of someone else.

- **Exceed others' expectations.** People who are really grateful for their opportunities go above and beyond.

Yes, I understand, sometimes implementing appreciation into our daily lives can be hard. And even sometimes we may feel that the world is against us and nothing is for us. However, I am in the game of small wins. I truly believe once you get enough small wins you will get a huge victory. Greatness takes time folks. Becoming the person that you truly want to become does and will take hard work. It will take major sacrifices, but these are the times that bosses are made. Bosses aren't born, they are developed. If one isn't grateful throughout his process, he will not become a boss.

A true boss respects the process, trusts the process, and doesn't rush the process. A boss has an extreme sense of self-awareness that allows him to learn from each situation he endures. the greatest gifts aren't things we can touch or grasp. The greatest gifts are the intangibles, the things we learn that help us become who we are.

One time while I was getting a haircut from my barber, we were discussing economics. I asked her should I get a cheaper apartment so I can save a little more money, or should I get a roommate before resigning my lease? She asked me, "Don't you live in a nice and peaceful area?" and I was like "yes, I do." Then she asked me, "Then why do you want to move?" I told her if I move to the cheaper area, I would be saving an extra $140 a month if I actually saved all of it. She told me, "Bryan let's do the math. That is only about an extra $35 a week and in reality, you wouldn't save the whole $140 every month." Then she asked me, "Would you give up your peace and safety for $35 a week?" I told her no. Then she told me something I will never forget. She stated, "I feel like you are just trying to have a cushion and I understand, but sometimes we don't need a cushion we need to learn to sacrifice and stay level-headed. If you stay in the apartments you are at now, you will find more ways to get it because you have to. Also, you are learning to manage your money on a level that most people will never get to, so just be grateful for what you are becoming than what you are getting."

This conversation with my barber hit home. She made me look at life from a different perspective. I told her thank you multiple times. Once again, it's not always about what we are physically gaining from our situations, it is what we are intrinsically becoming that matters most.

I challenge you to just sit back and think about the times that didn't go as you would have liked it to. Think about the times that you lost a friend, a spouse, a business partner due to disagreements. Now really think about what you learned from it. Self-awareness is key to true appreciation.

Bosses are grateful because they are self-aware enough to understand that something was still gained even through the disappointment. Just be grateful for it all. I literally mean all. This world doesn't owe you anything, so when you are blessed with something of value, be grateful enough so you won't take it for granted. Lack of appreciation will always lead to a lack of happiness. Happy people are thankful.

It's funny because every time I start to feel myself becoming stubborn because what I planned isn't going the way I would like it to, I know something great is coming. After I failed the Master Social Work Licensing Exam for the third time, I knew that being a licensed social worker in the state of Texas wasn't going to happen for me.

However, the reason why I am now so appreciative that I didn't pass is because just two months after I failed the licensing exam for the third time, I created my own speaking brand named Bryan Humphrey Speaks. I booked my first five to six events pretty quickly. The thing I came to realize while speaking at those events is that I have to better me because the people I am speaking to are putting their trust in me. With great power comes great responsibility. In the summer of 2017, I quit drinking alcohol, I quit hanging out with certain people and going certain places. That summer is when I chose to evolve into the person that I have always wanted to be.

So even through some of our biggest disappointments and setbacks, we must be grateful. If we are grateful for the disappointments, we will look at our disappointments in a positive manner. This leads to true growth. I realized that God had other plans for me and I rolled with it. Look at where it has gotten me. I feel pure, I feel genuine, I feel king, I am king, I am a boss.

Appreciate the rejections and no's. They weren't for you anyway. Don't stress what didn't happen. God has a bigger plan for you if you just remain obedient. The no that someone else told you is to open up another door for you or for you to master your craft to a better ability. We must always be thankful regardless of where we truly want to be. If one can't be grateful where he or she is now, then does one really deserve more? Think about that.

Greatness comes from using what you have in your toolbox to get where you need to get. The more you appreciate what you have, the more you will utilize what you have. It's not rocket science. Life is actually pretty simple if you just remain grateful. Smile through the pain. Embrace the difficult times because it's in those times that your character and spirit and built. Think about all the challenges you have overcome, bad habits you have broken, and fears you have destroyed, without doing these things, would you be as strong as you are today? I know I wouldn't. I wouldn't even be close.

So, when God is sending me a sign that a storm is coming my way and there is nothing I can do to control it, I know it's time for growth. I am so thankful for all of the sacrifices I have made in my life. From quitting alcohol, stopping my player ways with women, completely cutting off some of my old friends who didn't know their true purpose in life, going to the gym five to six days a week, stop going out to strip clubs, waking up early every day when I could sleep in, staying in to write this book and pursue my goals when I could be out partying, eating basic dinners when I could go out and eat at fancy restaurants all the time like the majority of people in their 20s, all of these sacrifices I have made me into the man I am today. I said the "man." A real man appreciates what he becomes during the process instead of what he gets out of it.

I remember when growing up my parents had these two-hour talks with my brothers and I. The talks were just about life lessons, what we should do and what we should not to. So, instead of going out with some of my friends on the weekends, I was stuck inside listening to my mom and stepdad preach this super long message about something that could have been talked about in 15 mins. But why did they talk to us so long? Was it really that important?

At that time, I didn't appreciate what they were telling me as much because I wanted to enjoy my teenage years. Now that I am older, I realized that my parents really freaking cared about my brothers and I. They had those two hours long talks because they wanted to put us up on some real-life game. It wasn't any cute stuff that grade teachers will tell you about the real-world. It was some real deep stuff. I appreciate all of those talks, literally.

Everything that I truly agreed with I have applied to my life in some form or fashion. I didn't agree with them on every single thing. I am my own person. But I am so thankful for all the information that I learned growing up in that household. Now that I have applied the information they told me, my mentality is beyond my time. It's crazy because a lot of my family and friends tell me I'm an old soul. It's in those meetings, conferences, and talks you really don't want to engage in that teach you the most. It's crazy how life truly works, but I am extremely grateful for it all.

Don't just push past the pain. Appreciate it. I love the process and whatever comes with it. When you love something, you are thankful for it. Love what you are going through because what you are going through is for you and nobody else. Appreciate your own uniqueness, you are special just the way you are. Others will appreciate you more when you are true to self. You are different, you are not afraid to do what everybody else is doing, you are strong enough to say no, and you chase your dreams and not someone else's.

Do you really think people will be thankful for you being in their life if you weren't genuine? No, I don't think so. And yes, sometimes it's painful being ourselves. It's painful because if we acted out who we truly are, we may lose certain individuals in our lives. I'm not saying be the ignorant you and shout to everybody "I'm just keeping it real." What I am saying is, be the true you, but in excellent behavior. Oh yea, a true boss knows how to act at all times. And a true boss is always appreciated by others, even their haters. Now isn't the time to be afraid to be who you really are. It's time to be thankful for everything that has made you the person you are today.

Tell someone you care about "thank you." Do this as soon as you get the chance to. That person you care about may not be here tomorrow. When we appreciate the people around us more than ourselves, it produces acts of selflessness. Selflessness is the act of putting someone else needs over self. It's not always about you all the time. Be thankful enough for the breath in your body to ensure someone else life is ok. Embracing altruism is key to self-fulfillment. One cannot be truly fulfilled until one is grateful enough to share his blessing with others. This doesn't always mean financially.

A person can share their gift, knowledge, love, positivity, time, and ideas with others. It bothers me when individuals are only grateful when they are getting helped financially. If you are only getting helped financially, then your appreciation of others won't last long because money is a tangible thing. However, when someone helps you with the intangibles, you will forever be grateful for them.

Why keep lending you money when I can help you find a job, when I can help you with money management, or even create more sources of income. Come on now my brothers and sisters let's be honest. Would you be more grateful for someone giving you $500 to help you pay your rent or someone who helped you create another source of income for yourself that you would be making an extra $500 a month for the rest of your life? I'll definitely be more grateful for the individual who taught me how to create another source of income for me rather than the one that gave me $500 loan.

We have to be grateful for the right things because it's the right things that make us a boss. People appreciate the value of someone more than anything. One must be mindful of the way they live their life. People who hold the most value accumulate the most appreciators. So, become more valuable so others will appreciate you more. The more a person appreciates you is the more a person will be there for you.

When it comes to people being in your life, appreciation comes from understanding. One cannot appreciate someone who he doesn't understand. So, if one is in a relationship, business partnership, a marriage, or friendship with someone else and they lack understanding about a part of the other person, then they will more than likely lack appreciation about that part of the person. It's truthful to say that things don't last between two people not because they have disagreements, but because one lacks appreciation for the other, and in some cases, both. The lack of appreciation comes directly from not truly knowing what the other person desires physically, emotionally, financially, spiritually, and mentally.

We are naturally attracted to others who understand us. It's just the flow of life, which is such a beautiful thing. One's life cannot become beautiful until one appreciates it. Beauty is in the eye of the beholder, and one cannot truly hold on to someone they do not understand. If more people would seek understanding, the world would be a better place because more people would express appreciation. Regardless of what someone said about you, you need to appreciate who you are. Yes, even the stuff about you that you may not like. Someone else may understand the part about you that you don't like about yourself more than you. Therefore, if someone else can appreciate your flaws, so can you.

Appreciation breeds happiness. I truly believe we become happier people because we have more things that we are thankful for. Think about it. Get out a piece of paper and write down every person you are thankful for right now and then read the list every morning. This will make you become happier. The moment we self-reflect about all that we do have, we will start to focus less on what we don't have. You don't know everything you think you need to reach self-actualization and become a boss, but you do need to be thankful. Think about some of your co-workers who never seem to be happy with the job.

Regardless of what's bothering them about the job, if they expressed more gratitude, I guarantee the job wouldn't be as terrible to them. Don't get me wrong, some jobs will start to make you think why you are even working there. Trust me, I have been there. The last six weeks while I was working for the state of Texas, I asked myself every morning, "Why am I even here? It must just be because of the money and benefits." And I'm not going to lie I really tried to be grateful, but I just didn't feel as if it was working. I really tried! Sometimes in life, it's not what we are a part of that we will be grateful for, it is who we become. If you are a part of something that you just can't feel yourself actually appreciating it and being happy, then that's ok.

Every job isn't for you, every organization isn't for you, but the person you became along the journey is the beautiful part. However, here is the tricky part; one doesn't realize what he becomes from the job he can't bear to appreciate until he leaves the job. It's similar to a relationship; one doesn't realize what she becomes from the relationship she can't bear to appreciate until she leaves the relationship. Sometimes in life, we have to separate from whatever it is that is tearing down our happiness to understand what really makes us happy. If one continuously stays in situations that they aren't thankful for, they will never realize what they are really thankful for. All of this starts with knowing self and being self-aware of what brings you happiness, peace, and joy.

Don't pursue a career, dream, or goal if you won't appreciate it once achieved. Notice I said you. It is impossible to reach self-actualization when you are going after someone else's purpose in life. What is for you is for you. Once you realize the purpose of you being on this earth, you must live out your purpose like your life depended on it. I am extremely grateful for everything that has happened in my process. The good, the bad, the pretty, the ugly. One must be grateful for it all to become all that he ever wanted to become. The process of achieving greatness isn't some complex and confusing process. No, not at all. One must look at the bright side in every situation. Yes, I understand that sometimes this will be hard because one may be in the part of their process that seems like they are in their lowest of lows. One should keep in mind that it's in the lowest of lows where a boss is created, not in the highest of highs. We have to remember we won't realize what being at our lowest of lows has done for us until we get out of that situation. If you can still manage to look at the bright side at your lowest point, then reaching self-actualization is most definitely for you.

You deserve to become who and what you truly want to become. Whatever you are going through in your process of becoming a boss, if you haven't yet, start to appreciate everything. A boss expresses his gratitude every day in some form or fashion. Let's live life through our disappointments, but let's appreciate that God is giving us something to go through so that we can become a better individual. Boss Up!

CONSCIOUS

"We all self-conscious. I'm just the first to admit it."—**Kanye West**

Open your eyes. Are you really about what you say you're about? What have you actually achieved and what are you actually doing to make your wildest dreams happen? Being conscious leads to one being self-aware of self. Being self-aware is critical to reaching self-actualization. Nobody is perfect. We all have flaws.

When I was younger, I was very self-conscious, but not in the manner that I needed to be. What I mean is that I used to worry about what everyone thought of me and if someone didn't think of me well, I wanted to do something where that person could think differently about me. I pretty much came to a vulnerable state where I was living so much to impress and please other people that I put my own self on the back burner. But why? I was already born great! There are two types of self-conscious: an immature self-conscious and a mature self-conscious. It's not that deep, but it is important. A person who has an immature self-conscious state of mind, happiness is created through others approval and affirmation. Now don't get me wrong, it's definitely ok to ask others for their opinion of things sometimes, but just keep in mind that their opinion shouldn't hold more value of how you view yourself.

Individuals who have an immature self-conscious state will do things because it will allow them to have a lot of friends and company. When I used to drink liquor a lot, it was easy for me to have friends because most people in their 20s enjoy socially drinking, well most people do actually. I knew if I had alcohol on me, people would want to be around, especially in a college environment because everybody wanted to have fun. Now, is socially drinking wrong? Most definitely not.

The route I was going with alcohol wasn't a healthy route at all. Now that I look back at it, I have come to realize that I drank so much because I knew I would always have people around me and at that time my self-conscious was slightly immature. I was still pretty successful in life, but I didn't know myself fully. Therefore, if I wasn't busy with work or school, I wanted to be around other people. I guess at that time I needed that to affirm that I was somebody.

We are all conscious beings. The other conscious being has a mature state of conscious. This person doesn't mind telling people no, doesn't live above their means, doesn't date someone because they think all their friends would like this person, is generally upfront about what they desire and need, is comfortable with their self and doesn't act out of character when others are around. I am now a mature, conscious being. What about you? This conscious being won't allow you to have as many friends, but it will enable you to have more true friends.

Now if you have your own business/brand or in business, sales or marketing you definitely want to be social to increase your net-worth to increase your status constantly. Associates are different from friends. A mature, conscious individual knows the difference between the two. In order to be successful, we understand that we must have tons of associates, but we only need a handful of true friends to be at peace. When one becomes self-conscious maturely, one fully values his or herself. One knows other people will stick around in their lives because of who they are. One doesn't get all tied up when others talk down on him and express their hate about them.

To be honest, when you become conscious in a mature state of mind, you embrace your haters respectfully. You understand that your enemy secretly loves something about you. I challenge you all reading this book to start doing what's best for you and not be afraid to let go of old friends because you have outgrown them.

Are you working your butt off every day for a certain lifestyle or because you enjoy the person you are becoming in the process? If one wants to reach self-actualization, they must seek self-growth more than anything. If you are not growing, then you are dying. When one is seriously conscious of their habits, actions, and behaviors, it puts them in a different league. I am a seriously conscious person when it comes to myself. I am very aware of my current strengths, weakness, flaws, and my habits. I know what situations to put myself in and not put myself in.

Have you ever wondered why some people who have so much potential and skill act like someone who doesn't have much to lose? It's more than likely because they don't care enough or don't know how to act out their conscientious thoughts. These individuals understand that they have much potential and skill, but are just too lazy to put it into action consistently. So how does one put their conscious thoughts into action consistently? Below is a list of things you can do to help yourself act more consciously:

Write down your goals: This will bring you clarity and motivate you to take action. Also, this will allow you to see your progress visually.

Get around winners: When you are around individuals who are getting things done, this will naturally make you want to get things done as well. Also, winners will hold you more accountable for your actions than those loser friends you once had.

Tell others no: You don't have to say yes to everybody's invitation and propositions. Give yourself more time to focus on you.

Be upfront with other people: Verbalize your feelings and desires. For example, if you are trying to stop smoking weed and your friend asks you to hang out at a place you used to smoke at, you tell him, "I'm trying to stay away from weed and not smoke anymore. I need you to respect that" before you even meet that friend anywhere.

Workout more often: Working out consistently will enable you to become more aware of where you are physically and mentally. If you're conscious of your body, then you will act more consciously when it comes to your eating, drinking, and sleeping habits. People who work out consistently usually have more structured lives.

Practice positive self-talk: Tell yourself "I am beautiful," "I am great," "I am king/queen," "I am healthy," "I am smart," "I am special," "I am valued," "I am chosen," "I am worthy," "I am a boss."

If you do this enough, it will subconsciously replace unhealthy beliefs and thought patterns with healthier ones. So not only will you be aware of your potential and skill, you will feel worthy enough to act on it.

Express gratitude: Tell others thank you, compliment others, pray for yourself and others. This will make you feel fulfilled with your life which will allow you to go after things that really make you happy more.

The more we act on our conscious thoughts, the closer it will get us to becoming a true boss. You are already the person you want to become, you just have to bring it out of you.

How important is stability and growth to you? When we look on social media, we see many individuals living these inviting lifestyles, and we think they are living the life. However, we have to remember that social media are just videos and pictures. It doesn't necessarily mean someone is doing well or have a good amount of money in their bank account. I'm going to tell you this directly, people will front to make themselves feel good. Why does the millennial who lives with their parents going out to concerts, fancy restaurants, and exotic vacations? Now I'm not going to assume anything about anyone's situation. It isn't my lane to do so. But it bothers me when I see grown individuals I know personally on Instagram, Facebook, or Twitter living the time of their lives, when I know they are in debt, still living with their parents, and/ or can't keep a job.

Is the lifestyle more important than your own well-being? Do you have to eat out five to six days a week? Do you have to go on a vacation every three to six months? Do you have to buy a brand-new car? Do you have to go out on the scene every single weekend and blow money at the bars and clubs? I'm going to give you guys the answer to this question, no you don't. Now don't get me wrong if you're financially able to do all of this and still save and invest your money then do your thing. However, if you don't get it like that and you continue to live like you do, you will always be behind. True bosses don't fake it. We become it. A true boss respects his or her current status and doesn't go above and beyond to impress people they don't even know.

Being conscious will allow one to think ahead. It will help you not to live for the moment all of the time. It will help you see delayed gratification instead of instant gratification. I understand that some people have the mindset of tomorrow isn't promised, so I'm going to spend what I have today. But what if you make it to tomorrow, the next day, the next day, and the day after that? I believe every human being has the right to enjoy themselves. However, I believe that things should be done in moderation.

I know individuals that make 60k plus a year and can't even keep a couple of thousand dollars in their savings account, and their credit score is below a 600. So, think about it, if one makes 60k a year and is completely independent with their own place and car. And another person makes 40k a year and is completely independent as well, but they both have $2,000 in their savings account and a 585-credit score, then what is the real difference here? I'm pretty sure the person making 60k has a nicer car, and more beautiful place, and goes out to fancier places, but is that really a big deal.

So, before you get to brag about how much money you make, the real question is how much money do you have? What is your credit score looking like? Don't try to fool people because of your annual salary, if you are struggling living paycheck to paycheck still, then be upfront about it. It's ok, nobody is going to fight you for telling the truth about your actual financial status. When one is truly conscious, it allows him to understand that everybody doesn't have it all together like it appears. Once you realize this, you will stop comparing yourself to others and move at the pace which is best for you.

Your process belongs to you. Be conscious enough to understand why others are achieving like they are. However, be conscious enough to know that your journey to greatness will be different. Reaching self-actualization is a marathon, not a sprint. You don't have to live a lifestyle of someone who makes six figures if you are only making $20 an hour. And if you're making six figures, that doesn't mean you have to live super-duper fancy. People who stay on top are conscious enough to do whatever it takes to stay on top. It's simple folks. It's not rocket science. Extreme conscious is absolutely necessary to extreme growth. Don't play yourself. You are worth a prosperous life.

Be honest about where you are along your journey in life. Also, be honest about the steps you are actually taking to get to greatness. I think sometimes we get caught in how difficult life can be at times and we forget to stay aware of what's going on in this world. Being conscious allows one to see life for what it is and who they really are. No sugar coating, no nonsense, no games.

When one is conscious, it enables the individual to be more responsible in his or her actions and lifestyle. But let's keep it simple, the actions one makes will determine the type of lifestyle they live. If one wants a lifestyle of health and fulfillment, then one must make healthy and fulfilling actions. Self-awareness is vital to self- growth. It's crazy to me because I ask individuals sometimes, do you know who you need to be and what habits you should have to take your life to the next level? And most answer no. Take into consideration that I didn't ask what techniques and strategies they have to learn. I asked about habits and character. I think sometimes in life we jump the gun. We try to get ahead too quick by not understanding what it's really going to take. A person who is self-aware of his behavior and conscious about how well or not well their work ethic is are the individuals that can make it in this world.

Growth starts with being honest with self. If you know you are only working out one to two days a week, don't expect to look like a bodybuilder. If you know you are going out partying every night, don't expect to catch the person that's staying in and going to bed by 10 pm. If you know you are eating fast food four to five times a week, don't expect to lose weight. If you know you are sleeping your full eight hours a day and waking up at six or seven o'clock, don't expect to catch the individual sleeping only six hours a day and waking up at four or five, especially if you guys are in the same profession.

My dad always told me, "You reap what you sow" growing up and he still says it sometimes now. The numbers of goals you will accomplish over your lifetime will be predicated on the amount of work you put in to achieve it. Respect is earned and is never given, I don't care who you are. Be aware of that. Stay conscious about where you really are in life and what you are really doing to grow and improve as an individual.

It's ok to tell other people that you aren't ready for something. This is where being conscious kicks in. I understand that we have to expect the unexpected in life, but I'm not talking about being ready for an opportunity as in terms of resources. I am talking about in terms of character. If you have the dedication, discipline, and tenacity to go forth with an opportunity and you don't have the funds to do so, then I'm pretty sure someone wouldn't mind helping you out financially because of the person you are.

Consciousness is such a powerful concept, but it's not deep at all. It's simply knowing who you are right now. It's not about what you can handle. You really never know how much you're willing to get burned until you step your butt into the fire. It's about knowing the type of person you are.

Are you headstrong? Are you a faithful person? Are you a genuine person? Are you a committed person? Are you a disciplined person? Are you transparent? Are you a person that loves to be challenged? Are you a person that's consistent? If you don't have the right character traits to be a boss, then you don't deserve the opportunity. Point, blank, period. You are only setting yourself up for failure when you ask for a position in life that doesn't match who you are a person. Being conscious of who you are right now will be a correlation of what you believe is possible for you right now.

One must be conscious of what one is truly about. For instance, it's cool to be dressed nicely everywhere you go, but if you're late on your rent and car notes, then is your clothing attire really that important? There are still some individuals living on this earth that will invest more financially into their shoes and shirts than into decreasing their consumer debt and increasing their savings account. To each of its own, but if one were more conscious, he or she would realize that what they are doing is creating a problem. Debt builds from not caring or being conscious enough to value what's really important.

Now, I understand that new pair of Jordan's or tailored suit may have been more important to one when they bought it, but delayed gratification is what creates a true boss. We can't always get what we want when we want it. I don't even wish life worked like that because that would be defeating the true purpose of growth. As I stated earlier in this book, I am a very conscious person when it comes to the important things of life. What I mean by important are the things that are going to help you grow spiritually and economically. I would be darn to say that finances or economic status don't matter. I would be lying my butt off. Those things do matter; credit score, spending habits, money management, and building yourself in the marketplace. Now we have to remember that everybody moves at their own pace. So, to belittle someone else would be inconsiderate.

However, it's nothing wrong with one being conscious enough to hold himself and/or his loved ones accountable for their actions. We have to keep in mind that life is about handling your business, whether that business is spiritually, mentally, emotionally, financially, or even physically.

Being conscious will allow one to understand what it really takes to become stable in all areas of life. Yes, I know life can be hard, but any single human being can become stable in all areas if they decide to. Don't give up on achieving true greatness because it can get disappointing. You are worth freedom, you are worth stability, you are worth being a boss.

Being a boss requires very hard work. Don't get fooled by the attention and nice things. Life can be tough at times for everyone. However, a boss acts consciously enough to do whatever it takes to become free and stay free. I always tell my family and friend to just be mindful. Keep in mind what you are actually doing, and how much work you are putting in towards your dreams and goals. Being conscious enables one to accept disappointment.

One is self-aware of how much effort they have put in and knows what they deserve. Respect is never given, it's earned. Please, I'm begging to whom may be reading this book to please be conscious enough to know that you will only reap what you sow. My dad's favorite motivational quote I guess. Life isn't some board game or video game. Life is the real deal. If one doesn't remain conscious enough along his or her journey to greatness, one will get broken down. And I have been there before, being broken on the outside sucks, but on the inside is even worse. Be mindful enough not to let life break you. Yes, you can let it bend you, push you around, but stand your ground and make it happen.

Life is about taking the time to strategize and implement the concepts that are going to get you to the next level. Self-awareness is key. Mindfulness is key. Application is key. Being conscious will keep your engine running. I believe that life is such a beautiful thing if we take responsibility for our actions and hold our own selves accountable. Boss Up!

COURAGE

Attack your fears. Do what literally scares you. When I was younger, I looked up on the internet what the name Bryan meant. On one site, it stated that Bryan meant Bravery. I became so excited. Ever since that day, I believe that I am a brave person. Being courageous means having the aptitude to do something that you are afraid of. Now, let's be honest; we are all afraid of something. For some of us it's death, it's life, it's sobriety, it's change, it's success, it's failure, and so many other things.

I am afraid of not becoming the person I truly desire to be. In simple terms, I am afraid of not reaching self-actualization. Self-actualization will not be achieved without courage. I feel that it's healthy to face what's holding you back. I understand that some individuals just can't take the truth, even if you say it in the most appropriate way. However, from truth is growth. One must be bold enough to admit his or her mistakes, flaws and downfalls. One must be strong enough to speak to others about what he or she is going through. You should have the courage to know that you are not in this world alone. I'm not saying tell everyone your deepest secrets. What I am saying is, have the courage to seek help when needed. Some of us have too much pride.

Having too much pride will eventually lead to destruction. Have the audacity to ask for assistance whether it's emotionally, financially, spiritually, mentally, and/or physically. The person you ask should be someone you trust. Sometimes you never know, the person you ask could have been through a similar situation as yourself. Be courageous enough to take the steps toward a life change and self-growth.

Don't flinch. Be a boss and make life flinch. Once one understands that there will for sure be dangerous and painful moments in our life, one starts to live more bravely. I tell others I care sometimes to be dangerous. And what I mean is be the individual that is bold enough to go for what he or she actually wants. Honestly, why not? Why not be great? Why not be the person that God already made you to be?

You are already the person you want to become, you just got to have to be courageous enough to bring it out of you. Life isn't going to give you what you want. Boss up and go get! Nobody has time to deal with an individual who isn't serious about chasing their dreams and goals. I mean think about it, dealing with a childish grown individual on a consistent basis when you are a mature grown individual is emotionally draining. Of course, we all want to help others, but helping others can bring hurt if the person we are trying to help isn't just getting it. Have the courage to slow your roll. Have the courage to express yourself assertively to the person you are trying to help about how you feel. Some individuals I had to completely cut off from my life, but I couldn't do it until I became courageous enough to do so.

I don't believe that any human being is completely fearless, but if one can be fearless about more than fearful, then that's a start. I fear going back to my old habits. My biggest fear is the fear of self-destruction. As I stated earlier in this book, I hate losing, but self-destruction is something I'm scared to death about. Therefore, I have to be courageous. It's not a choice for me. I have to be bold, be brave, and have the audacity to do things that the average individual is scared to do.

Having courage has made me strong enough to go after things I once feared, it allows me to speak in front of a big crowd not knowing who will truly get the message, and it enables me to do what's best for me. One must have enough courage to do what is best for them even when it brings a degree of pain and suffering. But we have to keep in mind that one cannot grow without suffering. Embrace what you are going through. This will help you grow stronger. People say I'm a tough individual because of how I think and how I live my life. I don't believe I'm just a tough rock star guy. I simply believe I have the courage and I express my courage when I feel like it's needed.

Don't give up. It takes a person with courage to keep getting back up when the world is steadily knocking you down. I'm going to be straightforward with you. This world will knock you down, heck, at least a couple of times. But you have to press on. Success isn't supposed to be easy. Why do you think most people give up along their journey? Life can be hard at times with all the surprises, twists, and turns. It can get discouraging, but this is why one must be courageous. Matter of fact, if one wants to be a boss, being courageous isn't an option, it's a lifestyle.

Go for what you deserve and don't settle for anything less. You are worth whatever you have to go through to reach self-actualization. Yes, I know at times life can make us feel that we are not worthy, but I am telling you, you are. You are chosen, you are special, you are cherished, you are valued, you are great, and you are amazing people. Don't let life win this battle. Go get that victory my brothers and sisters.

Wishing is ok, praying is even better, but how does one work for it when all odds or against him? It's courage. Courage will enable one to withstand the scariest parts of your process. Some of us may consider this time "hell week." Some of the scariest things I've been through has made me such a stronger and wiser person. With courage, I now embrace the harsh reality of life. About a year ago, I was having a conversation with my dad, and he said, "Bryan, sometimes people just don't care, and it doesn't matter how right you are." This one hit home. This statement alone made me face the truth about life.

At first, this made me afraid to be a genuine person. I really started having thoughts of doing people just how they do me. It's a dog eat dog world right, so why not? However, sometimes we have to be courageous enough to kill them with kindness. Crazy, I know, but it's true. Being kind to others that we have to deal with in order to grow sometimes is a hassle, but if done with a pure heart will bring so much peace unto self. Let's be brave enough to live peacefully.

Here are some tips on how one can become more courageous:

- **Gain more knowledge:** read books, listen to audiobooks, watch informative/motivational videos on YouTube, and ask others more questions.

- **Be positive:** the more you believe you can do it, the better chance you will have at making it happen.

- **Take on challenges:** go for it! When life or someone else puts you to test, don't back down. Withstand it.

- **Get around mentally tough individuals:** the stronger your friends are, the stronger you will become.

- **Acknowledge you fear something-** don't have too much pride. Everybody fears something, and it's ok to let others know what you are afraid of.

- **Attack your fears:** this is one important thing to becoming a boss. In order to reach self-actualization, one must go after what scares him or her. Sometimes we are afraid of the thing that is going to help us grow the most.

Have the nerve to do it. Don't be a scaredy-cat. Be comfortable with being uncomfortable. Life is already crazy enough as it is. Individuals who reach self-actualization at some point of time in their life had to be courageous. Be safe, but don't play it safe. This means be safe enough to have a backup plan if your initial plan falls into pieces, but at least give your dreams, your goals, everything your heart truly desires a chance. I'm begging you, if you do this, it will change your life. Have the courage to take a chance. Take a chance to become somebody that nobody expected you to be.

Shock the world; there is no reason not to. It's funny while growing up my mom called me nerve-racking, and she still does to this day. I understand why she calls me that. I'm the type of individual that is brave enough to do whatever it takes. Sometimes I'm like a chicken running around with its head chopped off. I will keep running until I get to my destination. Now that's courage. Having the nerve to pursue something that we don't have the slightest idea of how to actually get it done. If you always go for stuff that you know you can get, now is that really being courageous? Is that really living life? Our brain doesn't like it when we are courageous. Our brain is trying to keep us alive!

Challenge your brain. Challenge your brain with your heart and soul. For one to reach self-actualization, one soul should be exhilarated. One must totally enjoy their growth journey. When one acts out courage, it can be just as scary as the situation as one is in. Frightening! I remember my first speaking engagement at Fort Worth Western Hills High School in May of 2016, I spoke to over 200 graduating seniors. It was my first real speaking engagement ever! I'm not going to lie, I was very elated, but internally I was nervous as heck. I really didn't know what to expect. Thanks to my cousin in law, Mrs. Vanita Bell, for providing me with the opportunity. It was well worth it. Without courage, I wouldn't have gotten on stage and spoke how I did. Courage is needed to start something great, and courage is required to maintain greatness.

The real world doesn't always give us second chances, but God always does. Be bold and daring enough to trust God even in your lowest of times. Sometimes it's scary to remain obedient to the process, I'm not going to even lie. When other people in the world are living life young, wild and free, you are sticking to the plan like your life depended on it. Having courage builds faith. It allows one to be committed to something when all of the instant gratification isn't present. The human mind wants to be pleased.

As human beings, we want to do things that feel good to us. However, when one acts out courage, one is tough enough to sacrifice what they want right now to get what he or she wants later.

Think about individuals who beat cancer, who recovers from a life-threatening injury (spiritually recovery is most important), who becomes the first in their family to attain a master's degree or better yet Ph.D., and the ones who separate their self from the crowd and reach self-actualization. All of these are examples of courageous acts. Be lionhearted. Be a hero. Be completely unstoppable.

Be a Boss! Bosses do the stuff that others won't do. Bosses will step outside of their comfort zone and still do more than what's asked of them. If one isn't a boss yet, one should increase his or her level of courage to become one. It most definitely worth it. There is no need to let this real world break you into pieces like you have no value. Be courageous enough to stand up for what you believe in. I dare you to be brave enough to be different from your grade school buddies and relatives. I dare you to stand out and go get it!

Every level of growth requires a new degree of courage. If one wants more out of life, one must do more. I believe once an individual gets in tune with him or herself is the moment when one starts to do things they have never had the guts to do. Just have the guts! Have the guts to do something great! Everything great takes some amount of courage. It even took myself to have some courage to write this book. The average individual is not going to share his life stories with people he doesn't know, better yet the world. For one to change their behavior to become a healthier person, one must literally force himself to act differently on a constant basis. One must be courageous enough to act differently than how he feels or what he is used to. For example: if you are trying to break the habit of cursing, you will first have to find more appropriate words to replace the curse words that you say. Then you will have to hold your tongue and say words you know you are not used to saying. Things like this aren't easy, especially if you have been doing it for a very long time. We have to remember that without some change, there is no growth.

Have the courage to look yourself in the mirror and tell yourself I do. Have the courage to be committed to self. If one isn't committed to self, then one cannot truly be committed to anything they are a part of. When I started to break my unhealthy habits, I had to look myself in the mirror when I frightened my own self, and not in a good way either. Change can be scary. It can make us not even want to feel comfortable and secure in our own selves. This is why I tell people once you start your journey to self-growth and personal development, you can't stop. How one becomes secure of themselves when they are changing their ways to become a boss is to remain committed to the change that they want to see happen. We must understand that change won't happen overnight, but we got to have the courage to at least get started.

Are you willing to face the truth? A boss will face the truth even in times of difficulty or disappointment. Yes, a boss will feel the pain and discomfort, but that isn't enough to steer him away from continuing his process to reaching self-actualization. One can't get to the next level until one faces the bare truth of why they are on the level they are. The next level doesn't just require more work, it requires a better you. You may feel afraid of the step you are taking and all the new challenges that comes with it, but I know you can do it if you just believe.

Courage starts with belief. One has to believe that they are capable of doing whatever they are attempting to do. If a person doesn't believe in themselves to a strong degree, then doing something that is literally terrifying may be too much to ask. This is why I am in the game of small gains and big wins. Learn to break your goals down into manageable parts. Have the courage to tell yourself that the goal you set is too much for you right now. You have to do what you can before you can do what you want. One has to build himself up to the big event. It takes time. Then when you get to big event, you may still feel nervous and get goosebumps. Just because you have made yourself ready for the big opportunity doesn't mean you won't need the courage to step into your greatness.

Courageous individuals love pressure and pressure forms diamonds. The right amount of pressure will form a perfect diamond. Once a diamond has been formed, it can't be broken again. Becoming someone that can't be broken again will take extreme courage. It will take an individual to do things that they are afraid of over and over again. One has to be a little insane to do this. Be brave enough to bear on all the complications that you will have to endure to reach self-actualization.

The time is now. Go out in the world and give it all you got. There is no need to hold anything in. Have the courage to let it all out. If people call you extra, an overachiever, ADHD, OCD, or whatever other cute term that average people use to describe amazing people, then just know that you are on your way to reaching self-actualization, if you haven't already reached it. Achieving self-actualization is like driving on a major highway. You will experience traffic, car wrecks, detours, people with road rage, and sometimes a complete stop.

Becoming a boss isn't a smooth sailing trip, it's absolute chaos. The only way one truly gets through all the chaos to become great is to have faith. Faith and courage go hand in hand. Without having faith along your journey to greatness, courage is impossible. Faith is the opposite of fear, which is why you need it to do things you absolutely feel frightened about.

To the best of my knowledge, we only get one life on this earth. If you believe in God, heaven should be our next living environment once we leave earth. If not, you're probably still going somewhere. I'm not sure where exactly, but I know it's not earth. So, while we are on this earth, let's have the tenacity to put our thoughts into actions. Nothing great can be achieved without some sort of action. Faith without work is dead. Talk is cheap, and actions are expensive. And sometimes they are very expensive; they could cost us our life, our freedom, or bring us self-fulfillment and wealth. It's really all up to you. I will say one thing though; anybody has the capabilities of becoming a boss.

Yes, I said anybody. It doesn't matter your upbringing, your environment, if you have an extensive criminal background, if you are a single parent, if you lost your parents at a young age, if you have a past history with drugs and alcohol, if you have a history with not being faithful in your relationships, if you don't have a college degree or never got the opportunity to even go to college, and even if you are mentally or physically disabled, every single person can become a boss in their own form or fashion. You are already the person you want to become, you just have to bring it out of you.

Have the courage to stick to it by any means necessary. My main goal is to make this world a better place, but not by being some superman or earthly God. No, that's not me by a long shot. But just being able to serve others in the best way I know how. Being able just to spark other's mentalities is beautiful enough for me. If I'm able to change someone's life around here and there, that'll make me feel even more appreciative of life itself. However, none of the things I just mentioned can be sought out without courage.

Each trait I discussed in this book is essential to become the best you. Faith, Love, Confidence, Patience, Consistency, Perseverance, Competitiveness, Appreciation, Conscious, and Courage all correlate together in such a beautiful manner. Once you have all 10 of these character traits grounded within in your soul, you will become unstoppable.

You will become a diamond in the rough. You will become a rose that has blossomed out of concrete. You will become attractive to human beings of all nationalities and ethnicities. You will be respected by others. Others will honor you. You will be appreciated by others. And most of all, you will become a true BOSS!

BOSS UP AND GO GET IT!

Made in the USA
Columbia, SC
27 April 2018